CW00631684

YOUNG HORSE MANAGEMENT

PELHAM HORSEMASTER SERIES

YOUNG HORSE MANAGEMENT

REVISED EDITION

A. C. Leighton Hardman

PELHAM BOOKS · LONDON

First published in 1976 under the title
Young Horse Management by Pelham Books Ltd
44 Bedford Square, London WC1B 3DP
This revised edition published in 1987

British Library Cataloguing in Publication Data

Leighton Hardman, A.C.
  Young horse management.—2nd ed.—
  (Pelham horse master).
  1. Horses—Breeding 2. Horses—
  Training
  I. Title
  636.1   SF285.3
  ISBN 0–7207–1574–1

Printed in Great Britain by
Hollen Street Press Ltd, Slough, Berkshire

CONTENTS

ACKNOWLEDGMENTS

I should like to express my gratitude to the following people: Sidney Ricketts F.R.C.V.S., BSc, BVSc and Deirdre Carson M.R.C.V.S., BVSc for the very great help they have given me in reading and correcting large sections of this book; David M. FitzGerald for thinking of a suitable title; Mr. R. Boss and members of his staff for allowing me to photograph a horse they were backing. Yma Sherran and Stephen Riley for demonstrating the correct and incorrect methods of handling horses. Col. and Mrs. Coldrey for allowing me to photograph their horse at Herringswell Stud for the jacket cover. The diagram on page 104 is reproduced from *The Practice of Equine Stud Veterinary Medicine* by P. D. Rossdale and S. W. Ricketts and published by Balliere and Tindall.

NEWMARKET

A.C.L.H.

Foreword to the first edition

by Alan Lillingston

In ASKING ME TO write a foreword to her book, the author has paid me more of a compliment than perhaps she realises.

This book, I believe, should have a great future, and occupy a leading position amongst reference books on the subject of horse breeding.

It will appeal not only to the novice, as it deals most clearly and concisely with the elementary principles of breeding, but also to the expert as it contains a fund of information based on practical experience and intensive study.

In general, success in bloodstock breeding depends upon careful selection of the individuals involved, and then great attention to detail in the rearing of the offspring. The author's experience in the showring and as a judge, give her an excellent background to select for conformation. The manner in which her animals have been prepared for Tattersalls sales is proof indeed to me that she is a master of the art of rearing and preparing thoroughbreds for the sale ring.

At this time of general economic crisis, which is aggravated further in the bloodstock industry by enormous overproduction, only the most efficient commercial breeders with a truly professional approach are likely to survive. This book provides, in the greatest detail, many of the 'tricks of the trade'. If studied carefully and referred to when necessary it should be of tremendous value to all breeders.

Preface

*Y*OUNG HORSE MANAGEMENT describes the methods of handling and breaking young horses, covering the entire period from birth to maturity.

Before someone tries to break a horse for the first time it is essential that they practise on an older 'schoolmaster', which is well used to being lunged and driven in long reins.

A text book, however good, can only augment practical experience. The methods described in the following chapters work well for most horses but the reader must be prepared to adapt the system, at any stage, to suit a particular individual. If an animal is putting up serious resistance to its breaker, it is usually advisable to stop the lesson, rather than break the horse's spirit. Sit down and work out some other way of obtaining the same result in the end. For instance, it may entail leaving out one stage of the breaking programme.

Some youngsters, especially fillies, cannot tolerate the presence of a rein round their hind quarters. It is desirable, but not essential, that all riding horses are driven in long-reins before being backed. However, it is possible to make a mouth from the saddle, so rather than fight the horse, miss out the period in long-reins and back the horse once it is obedient on the lunge and accustomed to wearing a saddle. Very occasionally there is a clash of personalities, in which case a change of breaker is all that is necessary.

CHAPTER ONE

Notes on establishing a stud

IT IS NOT NECESSARY to own a large stud farm in order to rear horses successfully. A few acres and the right expertise will give equally good results. Breeders should keep a few top class mares rather than mass produce foals for the lower end of the market.

Stud farms should be located near to or in a horse-breeding area. Failing this they should be within range of a motorway or major trunk road. Buyers are notoriously reluctant to travel great distances to buy horses when they can find what they want within the small radius of a horse-breeding centre. Studs should be sited on good fertile land, in a chalk or limestone area, with a comparatively high rainfall and mild climate. Low rainfall areas are usually subject to periods of drought during the summer, when the grass burns up and the ground becomes rock-hard. In high rainfall areas droughts seldom occur and the grass remains green throughout the year.

Paddocks used for youngstock should be level to avoid accidents. Land which slopes steeply towards a fence can be dangerous, as horses may get injured if they are galloping downhill and the ground is too slippery for them to pull up at the bottom. On the other hand undulating terrain will develop muscles and teach young horses to be well balanced and adaptable.

Youngstock do best when allowed to range with cattle over a large acreage. Sheep keep pasture in good repair by treading down sods kicked up by the horses but they do compete for the shorter grass, also loose wool from sheep can create problems of choke or colic.

If small paddocks of 6 acres or less are used they must be planned so that the horses can be moved round the stud. Do not leave them in any one paddock for more than a month at a time and so avoid the risk of boredom and the land becoming 'horse sick'. Under this system cattle can follow the horses and help to keep the land clean and evenly grazed. Mixing species will also help to reduce the incidence of disease and unthriftiness usually found where there is a high continuing concentration of a single species in a given area. Only quiet breeds of cattle should be used for grazing with young horses; the most suitable breeds for this purpose are Herefords and Simmentals.

Where possible existing trees and hedges should be retained when laying out the paddocks, as large trees and shelter belts are essential but take time to establish. Open windswept paddocks will not produce well-grown youngstock or an early bite of grass. However, where no shelter exists, quick-growing non-poisonous varieties of trees and shrubs should be planted, at sufficient distance outside the paddock fence so that even the largest horses cannot reach them. Close-boarded fencing should be erected in particularly exposed places until the trees have become established.

Since horses poach wet land badly, paddocks must be well drained. For safety it is better to tile-drain all open ditches and fill them in completely. This will prevent accidents, particularly to young foals. Failing this, ditches and ponds should be very well fenced with at least 3 and preferably 4 or more rails.

Each year some young horses have their potential ruined through accidents caused by inadequate or dangerous fencing. Generally horses are a high investment commodity and therefore justify capital expenditure on facilities which increase their safety.

Apart from thick, high, stockproof hedges and substantial stone walls, the only form of fencing which can be considered safe for horses, is that based on the post and rail principle. Only wire fencing must be regarded as safe.

Post and rail fencing embraces a number of different forms involving widely varying levels of capital expenditure. The general concept is probably that of square cut wooden posts and rails, painted white, glistening in the sunshine on some

2

commercial stud farm. This undoubtedly is the answer where money is no object as it also increases the value of a property. However, other forms can be equally effective at less cost. From a general point of view they can be divided into three categories:

(1) Sawn timber posts and rails;
(2) Round or half-round rails and stakes;
(3) Man-made rails on timber posts.

Sawn timber posts and rails have the advantage of looking neat and tidy if erected well, but entail high maintenance costs. In order to preserve them, they need to be painted or creosoted regularly unless they were pressure creosoted; even then they rot with time. Sound rails withstand normal rubbing pressure, but will break on impact – for example, when a horse jumps but fails to clear the top rail. If fractured, the broken ends are often sharp and nails can be exposed.

Many horses like to eat untreated wood and will rapidly gnaw their way through painted rails. Wooden gates and rails are therefore normally protected by metal strips nailed to the upper surfaces of the wood. These are commonly put on in long runs, often the whole length of the fence. The strips themselves then represent a potential hazard. When a horse jumps out but fails to clear the top rail, the wood breaks but the metal strip holds firm. I know of at least one case where a young horse was killed through trying to jump out of its paddock and being caught on the metal strip nailed to the fence. It is therefore suggested that where metal strips are used for protection they should be put on in short runs not exceeding about 2–3 feet in length.

At least 3 and preferably 4 rails should be put up, where there are foals or small ponies, as these can easily scramble through or roll under a 2 rail fence. The rails must be level with the top of the posts to prevent headcollars being caught on the posts. When a horse feels trapped his instinct is to run back and if the headcollar or fence does not break first this can result in a broken neck.

Rails should be nailed to the inside of the fence so they cannot be pushed off the posts. To discourage animals from leaning on the rails in an effort to reach their neighbours, a double fence should be erected. This also helps to reduce the spread of disease on large establishments.

Unsawn posts and rails are often available in forestry areas. These are considerably cheaper to buy than sawn timber but since the rails retain their natural growth contours they do not look as neat. Locally available material can often be utilised for fencing, at low cost. For instance, old railway sleepers can be used as fencing posts, or with a certain amount of imagination, home-grown hedgerow timber can be utilised to construct a very safe fence.

Bearing in mind the high cost of maintenance involved with sawn timber rails, experiments are carried out from time to time with man-made materials. Those most commonly seen in Europe include aluminium and reinforced plastic.

Aluminium railing is made from white enamelled sheets moulded over 5 strands of heavy-gauge plain wire. The rails are kept taut by means of springs attached to the corner posts. They are not nailed to the fencing posts but pass through guides which are themselves nailed to the posts. This is the cheapest form of man-made fencing and requires no maintenance. When used for cattle, plain wire is placed between the rails but should not be used for horses. It has two major disadvantages: (a) it does not break on impact and could therefore injure a horse which, on jumping out of its paddock, fails to clear the fence; (b) it crinkles permanently under rubbing pressure. White flexible plastic may be used in the same way as the aluminium railing but is not as stable and requires twice as many posts.

Reinforced white plastic railing, as shown in the photograph below is preferred. This is more expensive to erect than the flexible fencing but does not have the same disadvantages. It remains rigid under normal rubbing pressure but will shatter on impact. It requires no maintenance, other than washing with plain water when it gets muddy, and it cannot rot. It is secured to the posts in much the same way as wooden rails, always looks newly painted, and is never gnawed.

When erecting paddock fences, all corners should be curved, not square, and never pointed. This reduces the risk of a bullied animal becoming trapped, pushed through a fence or injured by its companions.

Paddock gates should have their bars running vertically rather than horizontally. Horizontal bars can cause injuries when an animal kicks out and gets its hind legs trapped. To prevent this type of accident, it is suggested all paddock gates should be covered on the inside with Weldmesh.

Wicket-type gate fastenings are the easiest to operate when leading a horse, but should be reinforced with a large staple in the post and a spring clip attached to the gate by means of a strong metal chain. Low gates should have their height increased by attaching an extension to the top bar.

To save labour, mains water should be laid on to all the paddocks. The troughs should be fitted with automatic filling devices and have a plug in the bottom to facilitate regular cleaning. Water troughs should be sited well away from gateways to avoid adding to the mud in this area in wet weather. As far as possible they should not be placed under trees, otherwise they will fill with leaves, during the autumn. But at the same time they should be sited in a sheltered position.

When constructing buildings the following points must be considered:

(1) The length of time a particular building is likely to last. Inflation necessitates long life and low maintenance costs. Concrete block or brick construction is better than wood. American barn-type buildings with single-span roofs housing 4 rows of boxes reduce the overall cost of building construction, although adequate ventilation and fire precautions must be fully recognised in the design.

(2) The cost of maintenance. Low-maintenance buildings are essential. High-maintenance buildings can account for 25 per cent or more of the total running expenses of the stud.

(3) The best environment which will allow youngstock the greatest expression of their inherited potential.

New buildings must be so sited to counter the effects of the prevailing wind and take advantage of any sunshine. Southern aspects are therefore recommended.

Stress factors create management problems by lowering the well-being of stock. Buildings must be designed to give the best environment.

  (a) For comfort, the air temperature should not fall below

40°F (4°C); insulation governs condensation moisture and atmospheric temperature. In wooden buildings the roof and wall linings should be at least 2 inches (5cm) thick. The floors must be well drained and should be insulated, since up to 20 per cent of the horse's body will be in contact with the ground when it is lying down. A deep straw bed covering the whole floor gives most insulation and is therefore the warmest of all.

(b) Draught-free ventilation at all times is essential. Air flow should ensure that there is no condensation moisture or odour in the stables. Inadequate ventilation is a predisposing cause of respiratory infections. Good ventilation can only be achieved if there is a satisfactory air inlet and outlet. This is accomplished by fitting half-doors to loose-boxes which can then be left open, and by opening windows – the latter should be of the hopper type to carry the air up over the horses' backs. Outlets must be installed on the ridge to create adequate movement of air. Ionizer units may be used to clean the air.

(c) For maximum health animals require light as well as fresh air. Optimum window space is considered to be not less than 1 square foot (30×30cm) per 30 square feet (9×9m) of floor area. A 60-watt bulb gives sufficient light in a standard 12-foot-square (3.5×3.5m) loose-box.

(d) For comfort loose-boxes for horses should provide a minimum of 12 square feet (3.5×3.5m) of floor area, with an optimum of 15 square feet (4.5×4.5m). Weaned foals may be housed in less space but they will require as much room as an adult horse by the yearling stage, so it is considered uneconomical to build smaller loose boxes.

(4) The horses' health must be safeguarded and loose-box design should recognise disease control. Although grilles set in the walls between boxes may help youngstock to settle better, they also facilitate the spread of infection.

Floors should slope to an external covered drainage channel. An internal system carrying waste under a range of loose-boxes is a potential health hazard. Floors, and preferably also walls, should be made from a material such as concrete which is easy to wash down and disinfect. Mangers and water bowls should be designed so that they can be cleaned easily.

(5) Loose-boxes must be safe. Floors must be non-slip; when concrete is used this must be roughened. Horses can injure themselves if they become cast. Design should therefore include the following anti-cast factors:

(a) The junction between the floor and walls should be curved.

(b) Cement-rendered walls should have three 1-inch (2.5cm) deep ledges round the walls, the top ledge being 2 feet 6 inches (75cm) from the floor with 5 inches (13cm) between the other two ledges. This affords the horse some grip, enabling it to kick itself free.

(c) Mangers must be bricked or boarded in down to floor level.

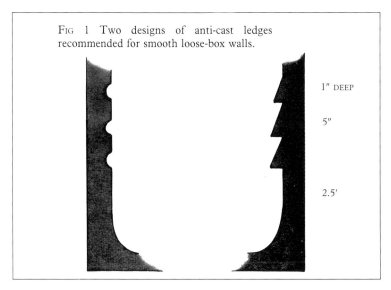

Fig 1 Two designs of anti-cast ledges recommended for smooth loose-box walls.

1″ DEEP

5″

2.5′

Since humans tend to lead horses in and out of doorways at an angle, all corners should be smooth and rounded otherwise hip injuries will occur. The doorways themselves should be at least 4 feet (120cm) wide and 8 feet (240cm) high; half-doors not less than 4 feet 6 inches high (135cm), with a wire-mesh grille over the

7

open top half of the door to prevent the horse from jumping out. Similarly windows must be protected with weldmesh. The free height inside the stables should not be less than 12 feet (3.5m) anywhere.

Electric cables, bulbs and switches must be protected and placed out of reach of the tallest horse.

CHAPTER TWO

Management of the young foal

Aᴵᴹ ᴛᴏ ɢᴀɪɴ the foal's confidence by quiet gentle handling. The earlier it is taught to lead the easier it will be. A first-size foal headcollar can be put on the foal the day after it is born; this must be clean and soft to prevent it from rubbing the tender skin of the baby foal. Since this size of headcollar is only worn for about 2-3 months, it should last for years if well looked after – but a word of warning here: all headcollars should be made from a material such as leather which will break under stress — far better a broken headcollar than a broken neck. If the weather is reasonably fine, young foals should be turned out daily from birth with their mothers. A sheltered paddock near the yard may be kept for this purpose. It can be very dangerous to let young foals run loose round the stud behind their mothers; therefore some means of restraint should be used until the foal will lead quietly in-hand. The best method of leading very young foals is for two people to hold a sack round the foal's hind-quarters and link hands across its chest (see Fig.2). In this way a young foal can be

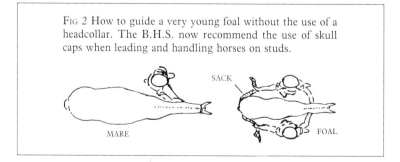

Fɪɢ 2 How to guide a very young foal without the use of a headcollar. The B.H.S. now recommend the use of skull caps when leading and handling horses on studs.

SACK

MARE

FOAL

(a)
CORRECT

(b)
INCORRECT

(a) Slip the rein through the leather strap at the back of the headcollar noseband. Hold the loose ends in your left hand. This way the rein will drop from the headcollar after a few strides, should the horse get away from you one day. A loose rein flapping round their legs will frighten most horses, causing them to gallop faster.

(b) Never wrap the ends of the rein around your hand − if the horse were to pull you off your feet you would not be able to let go.

guided anywhere in complete safety, the mare being led by another person behind the foal.

The foal should be taught to lead from its headcollar as soon as possible; initially this takes place in the loose-box. When putting the headcollar on, make sure that it fits reasonably tightly so that the foal cannot get a hoof through a strap, but not so tight that it will rub. As foals grow very rapidly and soon outgrow their headcollars, someone on the stud should be made responsible for checking at least once a week, to make sure that all the headcollars still fit correctly.

10

For the initial lesson in leading, slip a rein through the headcollar, get someone to lead the mare slowly round the loose-box and follow with the foal. The first time the foal feels a pull on the headcollar it will almost certainly try to run backwards, and if allowed to do so may rear or fling itself on to the ground, so a soft landing is essential. For this reason, never attempt to lead a foal for the first time in a concrete yard.

In order to encourage the foal to move forward freely, and prevent it from rearing place your right hand round the hind-quarters; do not twist the tail round. Keep your left hand on the rein and guide the foal round the loose-box behind the mare (see Fig.3). A few days later, once it gets the idea, remove your right hand and hold the base of the foal's neck. You will be surprised how much control this gives you and what a steadying effect it has on the foal. Young foals should never be knocked about or treated roughly, otherwise they may turn sour and become temperamental.

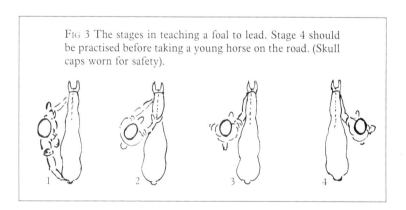

Fig 3 The stages in teaching a foal to lead. Stage 4 should be practised before taking a young horse on the road. (Skull caps worn for safety).

If a foal is lying down and you would like it to stand up, straighten its front legs out and then run your hand down its back bone. In the majority of cases, you will find that the foal will immediately leap to its feet. Should you ever have occasion to lift the foal never grab it with both hands under the stomach, as you may injure it internally. Rather put one hand round its chest and the other round its hind-quarters and lift. It sometimes happens that a newborn foal is frightened to lie down and will remain standing even when it is obviously sleepy. In this case hold the foal as described and lift it with its legs towards you, then place it gently on the straw.

A large covered yard is a great asset to any stud and might even be justified for a small private stud. The possession of such a yard means that all stock, including mares and young foals, can be given some exercise every day, regardless of the weather. The yard should be at least 40 feet square (12 × 12m) so that it can also be used for lungeing.

Exercise is essential for mares and foals – it helps the mare to clean up naturally after foaling and strengthens the foal's limbs. Therefore all foals should be turned out daily and left out for the whole day, unless the weather is very bad. Paddocks with high hedges and large trees under which stock can shelter when it rains, are ideal.

If a mare has been confined to her loose-box for any length of time, she will tend to gallop, kicking her hind legs in the air the first time she is turned out. This can be very dangerous; young foals have been killed or had their jaws fractured by being too close to the mare when she kicked out. Therefore these mares should be galloped on their own first.

To gallop a mare, use a very well-fenced small paddock — a close-boarded stallion paddock is ideal. Failing this, get a sufficient number of people to stand round the outside of the fence, so that they can turn the mare as she comes towards them. As soon as the mare is tired and stops galloping she can be led back to her foal, which will have been left — preferably held by somebody — in its own loose-box with the top door closed. Then both the mare and the foal can be led out. The mare should be walked round the paddock and allowed to graze until she appears settled; then the lead rein can be slipped from the headcollar.

While the foals are still young it is advisable to turn one mare and foal into the paddock at a time, allowing each pair time to leave the area of the gateway and settle before the next is turned out. Otherwise you will run the risk of getting the foals mixed up, since foals have to learn to follow their mothers and when young have a tendency to gallop off on their own and will often approach other mares when they get lost. For this reason it is better not to turn too many mares into a paddock together until the foals are nearly a month old.

For ease of operation a standard method of catching foals should be adopted and adhered to at all times. Any method which works can be used, but well-tried and satisfactory methods are shown in Figs. 4 and 5. Eventually you will find that the foals

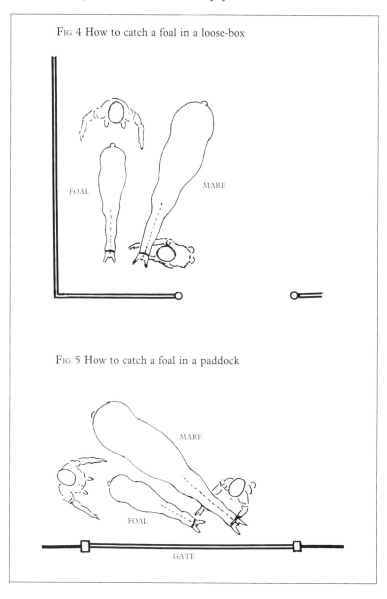

Fig 4 How to catch a foal in a loose-box

FOAL

MARE

Fig 5 How to catch a foal in a paddock

MARE

FOAL

GATE

automatically take up the position shown as soon as the mare is caught. In the paddock lead the mare up to the gate in order to catch the foal; if you try to catch a foal near the fence, it will probably attempt to jump through the rails.

When you first teach a foal to lead, it is advisable to take the mare and foal separately, getting one person to lead the mare in front, while another follows with the foal behind. As soon as the foal will lead really well from the headcollar alone, it can be led double with the mare as in Fig.6.

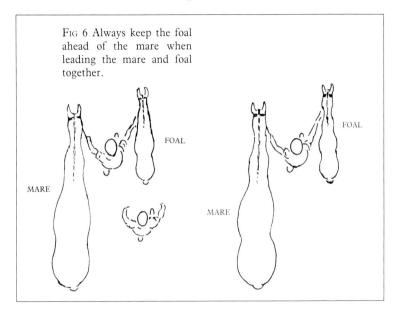

FIG 6 Always keep the foal ahead of the mare when leading the mare and foal together.

FOAL

MARE

FOAL

MARE

Initially, it is advisable to get a second person to walk behind the foal for the first week or so, until you are quite sure that it is not going to stop or run back. However, if there is sufficient labour available, foals are better led singly so that they can be schooled to walk out well from an early age.

When leading a mare and foal into a loose-box, always ensure that the foal walks in first, ahead of you and at arm's length, and allow the mare to follow behind, giving her the full length of the rope if necessary. It is not good practice to stand outside the loose-box door and let them go; this method teaches horses to rush in and out of doorways. At all costs one should avoid letting horses

14

catch their hips as they go through a doorway, therefore always make a wide turn into a loose-box and, on coming out, walk the horse in a straight line until you are well clear of the door-post, before turning. On no account should a handler hit a foal on its quarters as it passes through a door or gateway as this too teaches it bad habits.

When mares and foals are led out to the paddock separately, the person leading the foal must call out when he is ready to loose the foal; only then should the mare be allowed to go free. You may find yourself in trouble one day, if the foal runs back at the last moment, and the mare has already galloped half way across the paddock.

Foals are influenced by their environment as well as their genetic make-up. The mare plays a large part in shaping her foal's character and attitude to life. Since young horses are very impressionable, mares with stable vices such as crib-biting and weaving present a problem. The former can be solved if the mare wears a bar muzzle all the time. When the foal goes to the mare's head it encounters the muzzle, which teaches it to stay away from the mare's front end and hopefully never learns to windsuck. With the muzzle in place the mare cannot crib-bite.

Many Thoroughbred and Arabian breeders in England now leave all but their very young foals out all night. This is the generally accepted form of management on most pony studs and has much to recommend it for others. It entails a great saving in labour (sometimes as much as 45 per cent of stud expenses), as well as bedding and hay, which together amount to a sizeable annual sum these days. It is, however, essential that all foals are handled, and that they receive a feed each day. It is also vital that the mares receive a supplementary ration so that they can milk well and conceive again as soon as possible.

Under this system of management it is advisable to get all the mares and foals in before lunchtime and give them a feed while everything is quiet. While they are in, the owner or stud groom can examine each animal for signs of injury or disease and try any mares where necessary. It also means that a regular worming programme can be carried out and any routine veterinary or blacksmith treatment given. Also, manes and tails can be brushed out each day to keep them tidy, which is very important in the case of

15

show horses, particularly the native breeds and Arabs which are shown unplaited.

Foals must be accustomed to having their feet picked up before the blacksmith's first visit. This can be practised from the first day onwards. Face the rear, and with someone holding the foal. Don't run your hand down its leg as you would for an adult horse as most foals are ticklish. Place your shoulder against the foal to shift its weight onto the opposite leg and lift the foot. Since most foals feel insecure and frightened when first asked to stand on three legs, it is better to lift each hoof only an inch or so off the ground. Gradually increase the height as the foal gains confidence. Establish a routine from the outset; always pick the feet up in a particular order, then you will find that the foal will hand you each foot in turn without any need for lifting on your part.

It is essential that foals' feet are attended to regularly. Once they are over a month old the blacksmith should run a rasp round their hooves. Before this is done the foal must be walked out on level ground and its action checked carefully, so that any deviation from the normal can be corrected. Thereafter foals' feet must be trimmed every 2−4 weeks and their action and the shape of the feet checked each time for abnormalities.

Once foals are 6−8 weeks old, they should be wormed. Regular worming, at least once every 4−6 weeks, should then be practised for the rest of the animals' lives.

When foals have been handled and taught to lead soon after birth they seldom forget. If a foal is not handled for 9 weeks while the mare is visiting a public stud it may seem wild on its return. However, it will soon settle down and lead normally.

Those which have never been handled present a greater problem. They should be caught in a loose-box (which has first been bedded down covering the entire floor area), handled quietly and led behind their mothers as one would a new-born foal. Thoroughbred and Hunter foals are quite big at this age and will struggle to escape when first caught, so a strong, experienced handler should be selected, one who is unlikely to let the foal go. If the foal pulls back — grab a paddock rail if need be, rather than let it go. When leading place the loose end of the rein behind your back using your whole body to stabilise the foal. After the first struggle and panic, foals will normally stand quietly and with regular handling every day, rapidly become civilised.

Headcollars which are adjustable at both the nose and head-piece should be used. These are easier to put on in the first place, as they can be opened and buckled when in position, and they allow for finer adjustment as the foal grows.

CHAPTER THREE

Disease conditions of foals and young horses

Disease prevention is always better than a cure, and is cheaper in the long run. So wherever possible I will point out any preventive measures available to owners, as well as the symptoms and when it is wise to call in your veterinary surgeon. A quick guide to the symptoms of the various conditions can be found on pages 35 to 37.

Barkers, wanderers and dummy foals

These terms are used to describe obscure conditions sometimes seen in newborn foals. They are attributed to brain damage caused by lack of oxygen to the brain at the time of birth, or to infection by the germ *Actinobacillus equuli* or other organisms such as those which cause septicaemia.

Barker foals will often appear perfectly normal at birth but some time afterwards will show marked signs of respiratory distress and convulsions and in some cases will start to make a noise like a dog barking. If the foal is already lying down, it may jerk its head up and down and move its legs without being able to get up. If it is already on its feet it will probably show symptoms of blindness: wandering around aimlessly, bumping into the walls and continually calling for its mother without apparently being able to recognise her. Its ears may droop, it may rear and fling itself over backwards.

The foal should be placed and restrained on a blanket to prevent any bedding getting into its eyes which at the very least would irritate them, and at the worst cause blindness. The blanket should be placed under a heat lamp for warmth and an old sweater

18

can be put on the foal. Veterinary aid must be called in immediately before there is permanent brain damage.

Lack of oxygen at the time of birth, associated with premature breaking of the cord, or fractured ribs sustained at the time of birth, can cause these conditions. Foals with congenital heart abnormalities may show barker symptoms from the time they are born.

Wanderers and dummy foals are variations of the same condition. Wanderers, as the name implies, describes a foal which walks aimlessly round the loose-box, showing definite signs of irritability and restlessness. It will go off suck, chew incessantly or grind its teeth. Dummy foals on the other hand lose consciousness and become comatose.

These foals must be fed by stomach tube if they are to have any chance of recovering. This condition is more common in thoroughbreds.

Diarrhoea or Scouring

This can be a symptom of several diseases, errors in feeding or worm infestations.

Most foals will suffer from diarrhoea at some period before they are weaned, often when the mare comes in season after foaling. This is thought to be due to changes in the composition of the mare's milk at this time. The ingestion of poor quality high-fibre feed, such as inferior hay, before the foal's digestive tract is capable of dealing with these substances, may play a part. The foaling heat scour usually stops quite naturally soon after the mare has stopped being in season. The foal does not go 'off suck' or show any other symptoms of illness but this 'natural' scour can weaken the foal and make it more susceptible to infectious scours at this time.

When foals scour, the tail and adjacent areas should be washed at least once a day and some Vaseline smeared round the hind-quarters, to prevent temporary baldness. This is especially important if you intend to show or sell the foal before weaning.

All infectious diarrhoeas should be isolated and have immediate veterinary attention, as young foals have very few reserves and are soon pulled down in condition.

When foals scour there is usually a characteristic odour which

19

is immediately recognisable on entering the loose-box. The foal's temperature is usually raised. The thermometer must be held against the side of the rectum otherwise, in cases where the rectum is relaxed, a false reading might be obtained. The foal may go 'off suck', or may continue sucking. Some foals drink large quantities of water and their stomachs become distended. Foals which stop sucking soon become dehydrated, and in these cases fluids and a balanced electrolyte mixture such as Stat must be given. On no account should water be restricted. Signs of dehydration usually include sunken eyeballs, staring coat and a weak pulse.

Draughts and sudden changes in temperature can be predisposing causes of scouring. When it occurs the most important thing to remember is that any fluid loss must be replaced and the electrolyte balance maintained. If the fluids are not replaced in adequate amounts the foal will die as a direct result of fluid loss. The foal's tongue will often become coated and there is a marked loss in condition and wasting of the muscles.

Injecting some serum from the mare into the infected foal will often aid recovery, due to the antibodies this serum contains. Antibiotic treatment is usually necessary for recovery.

Entropion

Describes a condition in which you will notice that the foal has a chronic watering of one or both eyes. This becomes apparent as early as one or two days after birth. On careful examination one can see that the bottom eyelid has turned inward and the lashes are irritating the eye, causing inflammation of the cornea.

This is a job for your veterinary surgeon and he may wish to insert some stitches into the bottom lid, which will have the effect of making the lid turn outwards in the normal manner. The stitches are usually left in place for about 2 weeks.

Equine Infectious Anaemia (Swamp Fever)

This is a notifiable disease of horses and any suspected case must now be reported to the police or Ministry of Agriculture. It normally occurs in low-lying swamp areas—hence its name—and is transmitted by mosquitoes. It is endemic in the U.S.A. and with the increase in the traffic of horses throughout the world, diseases such as swamp fever are likely to occur almost anywhere. A case was reported for the first time in England in 1975.

This disease can manifest itself in several different ways:

(1) fever associated with anaemia, minute areas of haemorrhage on the undersurface of the tongue and soft swellings on the limbs and other parts of the body, sometimes loss of condition;

(2) chronic loss of condition together with anaemia, ending in the death of the animal;

(3) sudden death without any prior symptoms.

Some affected animals do not show any symptoms unless they are subjected to stress such as foaling. These animals can nevertheless transmit the disease to other healthy stock, given the right conditions.

Diagnosis of the disease is made by taking a blood sample and subjecting it to a special laboratory test known as the Coggins test.

In the United Kingdom no compensation is paid for affected animals, which, if kept, must be isolated for the rest of their lives.

Guttural Pouch Tympanitis

This is a very rare condition sometimes seen in foals. The affected animal appears as in Fig.7, with a large swelling in the region of the guttural pouch. When pressure is applied to the swelling, air is driven out but the swelling returns within a few hours.

The affected animal makes a roaring or snoring noise when breathing and often makes more noise when eating. In hot weather the foal may be distressed. There may or may not be a nasal discharge. This condition might be inherited or it can be due to an infection. Immediately you see the first symptoms you should call in your veterinary surgeon; he may advise an operation. On no account should you attempt to lance the swelling yourself or let any fluid or air out, as this could start up a serious infection.

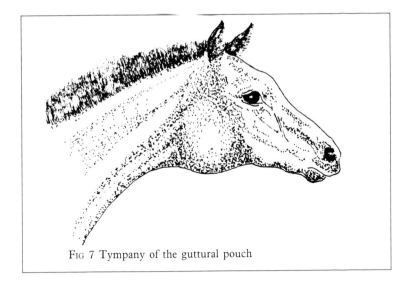

FIG 7 Tympany of the guttural pouch

Haemolytic Disease

This is a blood disease of the newborn foal in which the chief symptoms are anaemia and jaundice. The disease is caused by a blood group incompatibility between the foal and its dam, and is somewhat analogous to Rhesus babies in human medicine.

The condition arises when a foal, while still in the womb, has inherited a blood group from its sire which is incompatible with the dam's blood. The mare then becomes sensitised to this 'foreign' blood group and produce antibodies against it. She concentrates these antibodies in her colostrum so when the foal first sucks they pass into its bloodstream. The antibodies then combine with and destroy the foal's red blood cells, which results in severe anaemia and jaundice.

If you own a mare which has previously had a foal with haemolytic disease or if you want to make sure that your mare does not have a foal with haemolytic disease, then about 3–4 weeks before she is due to foal ask your veterinary surgeon to take a sample of her blood. This sample will be laboratory tested and compared with samples taken during the following 2 weeks to see if there is any increase in antibody level. Any significant increase would denote that the foal will be at risk should it receive colostrum from its own dam.

22

If it has been determined that the mare has an increased antibody level and that the foal when it arrives will therefore be at risk, the main preventive measures to be taken are:

(1) Obtain a foal-size muzzle — this must be put on the foal the moment it gets to its feet, to prevent it from drinking any of its mother's milk and must be left on for 36 hours. If all access to the dam's colostrum is withdrawn the disease cannot occur.

(2) As the foal must have some colostrum an alternative supply must be provided. This can be obtained at any time from another unsensitised foaling mare and kept in a deepfreeze until needed. It should be warmed to blood heat before feeding. Thoroughbred foals should receive 500ml.

The mare must, of course, be milked out at least six times a day to prevent her from drying up before the foal is allowed to suck. This milk *must* be thrown away.

The clinical signs of haemolytic disease are that the foal will be seen to yawn, appears sleepy and short of breath due to lack of oxygen in the blood, which in turn is due to the destruction of the red blood corpuscles. The mucous membranes are yellow. This condition usually becomes apparent within the first 36 hours after birth, but may occur later.

Hernia

A hernia or rupture is caused by incomplete development of a muscle wall (usually abdominal) and the protrusion of an organ or its fatty connective tissue through the hole which has been formed, causing a swelling to the outside beneath the skin.

Umbilical hernias are the type most commonly met in foals. They usually appear at about 6 weeks of age and are seen as a swelling in the navel region due to part of the bowel protruding through the umbilical ring, which has failed to close up in the usual way.

This type of hernia should not be confused with thickening, which sometimes takes place in the region of the navel. This is hard and unyielding, whereas in the case of a hernia a distinct ring can be felt through which the protruding mass can be pushed back into the abdomen, and through which it protrudes again once the pressure is released.

An umbilical hernia is sometimes self-curative and tends to disappear quite naturally as the animal gets older, but in some more severe cases treatment to close the hernia ring is necessary. This should be done at about 4 months old, before weaning.

A lamb ring is applied with care by a veterinary surgeon and left in place until its drops off. This form of treatment is very effective, with a minimum of inconvenience to the foal.

Equine Influenza

Affected horses will cough, run a temperature and sometimes have a slight nasal discharge, Adult horses usually recover in about a week, but young foals often become seriously ill and some die, as they have very little resistance to influenza at this early age unless the mare has been vaccinated recently, before foaling.

The incidence of influenza among foals can be greatly reduced by ensuring that all brood-mares are vaccinated annually and that the booster vaccination is carried out in the last month of pregnancy. This will produce the maximum amount of antibody in the mare's colostrum. No ill effects as a result of vaccination, either to the mare or the foal she is carrying, have ever been recorded. Foals should be vaccinated at 3 months and again at 4 months, with a booster dose every 5-7 months.

As far as Thoroughbred yearlings are concerned, it is recommended that the booster vaccination should take place in July or August.

Joint ill or Navel ill

This condition usually becomes apparent some time between 5 days and 4 months of age, but most commonly at about 3 weeks. It is characterised by swellings in the leg joints or around the navel. The foal is usually lame in the affected limb or limbs.

The germs which cause this disease are thought to gain entry at the time of or soon after birth. Maximum cleanliness should therefore be observed at foaling time.

The foal may also go 'off suck' and appear dull and listless, the temperature rising to $103° - 105°F$ ($39.4°40.6°C$). It will tend to spend most of its time lying stretched out flat on its side. One or more leg joints may appear swollen, tense and hot. If left untreated these will eventually burst, discharging bloodstained material, and the foal will gradually get weaker and may die. Sometimes abscesses are also found on the internal organs, in which case death usually occurs.

Prevention mainly consists of maintaining scrupulously clean surroundings at foaling time and a liberal application of wound powder such as Acramide to the cord the moment it breaks. This should be repeated an hour or two later. Make sure the foal receives some colostrum within the first 24 hours of birth, particularly in cases where the mare has been running her milk before foaling. The mare's colostrum and foal's serum can be checked for antibody level. As a final precaution the foal should be given antibiotic cover for 3 consecutive days after birth.

Should you suspect that your foal has Joint Ill, call your veterinary surgeon immediately, as if left untreated, at the very least there may be some permanent damage to the foal's joints.

Meconium Colic

Meconium is the brown or black fairly hard excretory material which collects in the bowels before birth. It should be passed within a few hours, helped by the purgative action of the colostrum. The meconium is thought to consist of amniotic fluid cells, bile and debris from the intestines which have collected before birth.

It is very important that the meconium should be passed within a few hours of birth to allow normal digestion to take place. If the meconium is retained, colic will occur. The foal will probably carry its tail higher than normal, and may be seen standing in a crouched position with its back arched, straining. In a more advanced stage it will show very definite signs of colic: kicking up at its stomach, rolling and even lying on its back with its legs tucked up against its stomach in an effort to relieve the pain.

Retained meconium and constipation in the foal may be due to a costive diet and lack of exercise in the mare.

A dose of liquid paraffin by mouth or an enema of warm soapy water does sometimes help to relieve this condition, but it is probably better to call in your veterinary surgeon as soon as you notice the first symptoms, rather than wait until the foal gets worse. Routine dosing of all newborn foals with liquid paraffin by mouth can help to prevent meconium colic.

This condition appears to be more common in colt foals than fillies, especially overdue colt foals.

Meningitis

This is the term used to describe inflammation of the membranes covering the surface of the brain and/or spinal cord.

The affected foal usually goes 'off suck' and appears generally ill, with temperature, respiration and pulse higher than normal. It may become dazed and walk into objects in its path, and develop convulsions.

Veterinary help should be called in immediately as this is a very serious disease and only careful nursing can effect a cure.

Pervious Urachus

Describes a condition in which a continuous trickle of urine will be seen coming from the navel within the first 4 days. It will probably remove the hair from the lower regions of the hind legs, unless these parts are smeared with Vaseline.

Before birth the foal lies inside a sac known as the amnion and is immersed in amniotic fluid. This is surrounded by the chorio-allantoic membrane, which contains allantoic fluid, the foetal urine which has collected before birth. The foal's urinary bladder opens directly into the chorio-allantoic sac, which gradually fills with urine, thus preventing over-distension of the bladder. At birth the umbilicus normally closes.

In the case of pervious urachus there is still direct access for the urine through the navel cord to the outside. The condition will sometimes cure itself, but if it does not soon improve your veterinary surgeon should be called as treatment may be necessary. Swabbing with 10% Formalin solution is often recommended.

Pneumonia

This is inflammation of the lungs with a resulting breakdown of lung tissue which greatly impairs respiration. Respiration is faster and deeper than normal. A variety of germs, bacteria and viruses are able to cause pneumonia in susceptible foals.

Predisposing causes of pneumonia may be exposure to cold, wet

26

weather, or stuffy and badly ventilated stables. It can also be produced by careless drenching — allowing some of the fluid to go down into the lungs, which is always a risk.

Possible symptoms of pneumonia are a high temperature and fast, laboured breathing. The foal will go 'off suck' and there may be fits of shivering and some nasal discharge. Careful nursing and management is all-important as a relapse can take place at any time if the standard of care is relaxed.

Veterinary aid must be called in right at the beginning if a good chance of recovery is to be expected.

Summer pneumonia: This is a highly infectious disease of young foals from about 1–4 months old, caused by the germ *Corynebacterium equi.* As its name implies this condition is most often seen during the summer months. It is more commonly found in Scandinavia and Australia but outbreaks do occur from time to time in the British Isles.

The germ causes areas of pus (abscesses) to form in the lungs. By the time symptoms of pneumonia develop the disease is usually fairly well advanced; hence the high death rate.

Antibiotic treatment by your veterinary surgeon and good nursing give the only possible chance of recovery. Foals with pneumonia of any type should be isolated immediately, as summer pneumonia can spread very rapidly through a stud.

Respiratory Infection due to Herpes virus

This virus causes a respiratory infection most commonly seen in yearlings. Under certain conditions it also causes abortions in mares, and occasionally produces signs of paralysis.

In young horses the symptoms are usually those of a common cold: nasal discharge, sometimes accompanied by a slight rise in temperature, reddening of the mucous membrane in the eyes (conjunctivitis) and swelling of the glands in the angle of the jaw.

It usually clears up on its own, but where there is a rise in temperature, however slight, your veterinary surgon should be consulted. (See also Snotty noses, page 30.)

Round joints

These are the result of inflammation affecting the growth plates (epiphyses) immediately above or below the knee and fetlock

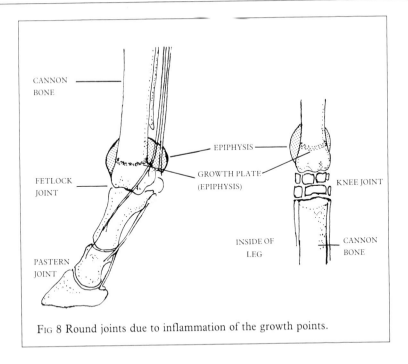

CANNON
BONE

EPIPHYSIS

GROWTH PLATE
(EPIPHYSIS)

FETLOCK
JOINT

KNEE JOINT

INSIDE OF
LEG

CANNON
BONE

PASTERN
JOINT

FIG 8 Round joints due to inflammation of the growth points.

joints of yearlings and foals. They are usually caused by trauma or errors in diet such as an excess of phosphorus and too little calcium in the ration, or lack of vitamin D (the sunlight vitamin). They can occur when a high-energy diet is being fed to produce heavy-topped fat animals, or when the ground is hard.

The swellings are hot and tender and the affected animal may go lame. Later they will appear firm and cold. 'Knobbly fetlocks' are quite commonly seen in thoroughbred foals between 3 and 6 months of age, and they usually come right in time (see Fig.8). Swellings involving the area above the knee or hock joints are more common in yearlings.

Treatment usually consists of correcting the diet, and reducing the animal's body weight where necessary.

Ruptured bladder

This is a rare condition, probably due to some inherited weakness in the bladder wall.

The symptoms are similar to those of meconium colic, except

28

that affected foals often scour, and it usually becomes apparent around the third day. The foal's stomach becomes distended with fluid and it may only be able to pass very small quantities of urine.

Your veterinary surgeon should be called in immediately this condition is suspected, as an operation will be necessary to repair the tear in the bladder wall.

Exercise is normally restricted after abdominal surgery. However mares can still be turned out for an hour or so on warm days and receive some grass and exercise if the foal is put in a round cattle forage feeder, placed in the middle of a paddock. The metal sides should be enclosed with plastic netting to a sufficient height so that the foal cannot jump out. The feeder is first placed on its side and then lowered over the foal, or it may be adapted by your blacksmith to include a door.

Salmonella

As with calves, if not treated with antibiotics from the outset this is a highly infectious killer disease of foals. It causes epidemics of scouring on studs.

The symptoms usually consist of a watery, bloodstained diarrhoea, very high temperature, colic and rapid breathing.

Veterinary aid must be called in immediately this disease is suspected, and any affected foals isolated. Loose-boxes which have housed sick foals must be very thoroughly disinfected, under the guidance of your veterinary surgeon, before any further foals are put into them.

Septicaemia

In this disease, bacteria have somehow managed to gain entry into the foal's bloodstream, where they circulate round the body and invade any or all of the vital organs. A predisposing cause of this disease can be lack of colostrum and thus the antibodies against disease which it contains. In most cases the affected animal dies; the course of the disease is often very short. It usually occurs within the first 4 days of life.

Sometimes the only symptoms noticed are a high temperature and general signs of illness followed soon afterwards by death. The earlier a veterinary surgeon can be called in the more chance he will have of saving the animal's life.

Shaker foals

This is a condition sometimes encountered in young foals 3 – 8 weeks old. The disease appears to be peculiar to America — only one case has been reported in England to date.

The condition is rapid in onset. The affected foal is usually found lying on its side, unable to rise without assistance. When helped to its feet, it will usually start to suck normally but muscular trembling (shaking) soon occurs and the foal will drop to the ground. Death usually follows in about 72 hours. The exact cause of this syndrome is obscure at the moment but veterinary aid should be called the moment the condition is suspected.

Sleeply foal disease

Describes a disease caused by the germ *Actinobacillus equuli*, and usually becomes apparent 2 – 4 days from birth.

The affected foal appears dull and may go 'off suck'; the temperature may be sub-normal. After several hours the foal appears sleepy (hence the name) and may show signs of colic and diarrhoea or develop convulsions.

This organism usually attacks the kidneys and brain.

The sooner veterinary aid is called the greater is the foal's chance of survival.

Snotty noses

This is usually caused by a virus infection accompanied by a secondary bacterial infection. Affected horses have a runny nose, sometimes cough and run a slight temperature. Their glands may be enlarged.

It usually clears up on its own, but a veterinary surgeon should be called if there is any rise in temperature.

A predisposing cause is badly ventilated stables. Horses with snotty noses should not be worked until the condition has cleared up.

Strangles

This is a disease more commonly seen in young horses up to five years old. It is caused by the germ *Streptococcus equi*, is very highly contagious and will cause the death of young foals. Incubation is usually from 2 – 14 days. Infected horses show a rise in temperature, appear dull and go off their feed. They often have a cough, sore throat, profuse discharge from the nostrils and swellings in the angle of the jaw. This causes the horse to hold its head and neck out stiffly. After a few days an abscess will form in the swelling, mature and finally burst, discharging bloodstained pus. This pus and the nasal discharge are highly infectious, so very great care should be taken that anyone handling an infected horse does not come in contact with other unaffected horses at this time. As soon as the abscess has burst the temperature usually becomes normal and the swelling subsides. Recovery is usually complete in a few weeks.

Treatment consists of immediate isolation of the affected animal and calling in your veterinary surgeon, who may wish to treat the animal with antibiotics.

Tetanus (Lockjaw)

This disease affects horses of all ages but its incidence among young foals can be reduced to a very great extent by giving a mare which has already had primary tetanus toxoid injections a booster injection about 3 – 4 weeks before foaling. She will then produce antibodies which will be transferred to the foal in the colostrum, giving it immunity to tetanus for the first few weeks of its life. Immunity can be maintained up to about 3 months of age by giving an injection of tetanus anti-serum at 6 weeks of age.

This disease is caused by the germ *Clostridium tetani,* which can survive for long periods in a dormant state outside the human or animal body. It cannot live in the presence of atmospheric oxygen. The germ normally gains entry through deep wounds, such as in the feet, deep puncture wounds, or through the navel at the time of birth, i.e. any site not immediately in contact with the atmosphere.

The germs do not leave the site of entry but produce a toxin which they release into the bloodstream. This acts on the central nervous system, producing symptoms of paralysis.

The horse shows unusual signs of nervousness. He will stand with his limbs stiff, tail raised stiffly, head and neck stretched out and ears pricked. If the head is raised quickly the third eyelid (haw) will flick across the eye very noticeably.

If tetanus is suspected your veterinary surgeon must be called immediately.

31

The preventive measures available are:

(1) *Tetanus serum* — is fast acting but provides immunity for about 4 weeks only. It has fewer side effects than tetanus toxoid and is consequently invaluable for administration to very young foals. It is also used after accidents and operations to give animals which have not been vaccinated against tetanus temporary passive immunity to the disease while at risk.

(2) *Tetanus toxoid* — is slower acting and is used to give lasting, immunity. It is given at 3 months, with a second injection 1 month later. This is followed by an annual booster injection a year later.

Warts (Milk warts or grass warts)

These warts appear as clusters of small skin-coloured lumps on the muzzle and lips of young horses. They are commonly seen in yearlings at grass during the summer — hence the name 'grass warts'.

They usually disappear on their own after 2 – 3 months without treatment. That is as soon as the affected animal has developed immunity to the virus infection which causes the warts.

Developmental abnormalities

Foals, like babies, can be born with various weaknesses and deformities including 'parrot mouth', cleft palate, hernia, and deformed limbs, (see Plate 6). Some of the more common limb deformities are:

(1) *Over-long weak pasterns:* in these cases the foal walks with its fetlocks touching or almost touching the ground. The condition usually rights itself as the foal becomes stronger. Most cases of limb weakness in young foals respond to long periods of exercise in the paddock.

Since the fetlock is touching the ground it will become very sore if protective bandages are not applied. Care should be taken that the joint does not become infected, otherwise an infective arthritis (Joint Ill) might result. Once the fetlock has come up off the ground the bandages may be dispensed with but any sore places should be treated with an antibiotic spray, some of which also have the effect of hardening the skin.

(2) *Contracted tendons:* the foal may only be able to walk on the tips of its toes, or in very bad cases be entirely unable to rise. If the contraction is very bad the foal may have to be put down, but in some cases an operation to cut the tendons and straighten the leg may be successful. In other cases splinting the leg may work well.

(3) *Knock knees, twisted fetlocks etc:* When foals are born with bent legs which do not begin to straighten within a week of birth, or where their legs start to bend soon after birth, your veterinary surgeon should be consulted, as the longer these weaknesses are left the harder they are to correct. Correction must take place while the foal is still growing, and may take the form of plaster casts. In some cases a leg which is growing unevenly may need to be stapled to straighten it but this is a major operation, so the value of the foal must be taken into consideration first (see Fig.9). Feet which turn in or out from the fetlock joint can usually be corrected quite satisfactorily by the blacksmith. Any minor deviation can usually be rectified by careful trimming but any major fault will probably need special shoeing from the moment the foal's hoof can take a shoe (usually at 8 weeks of age). The

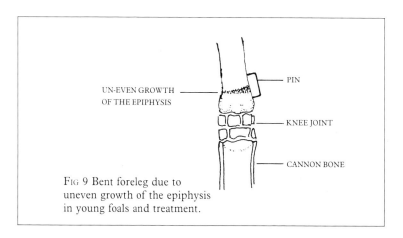

UN-EVEN GROWTH OF THE EPIPHYSIS

PIN

KNEE JOINT

CANNON BONE

Fig 9 Bent foreleg due to uneven growth of the epiphysis in young foals and treatment.

33

outside of the shoe is built up to turn the toe out, and the inside built up to bring the toe in. More slip can be achieved if the front of the shoe, at least, is smooth. Corrections to any joint must be made gradually, otherwise an enormous strain will be placed on the affected limb.

Developmental abnormalities may be inherited or they may be due to environmental conditions.

Wobblers

Describes a condition more commonly seen in colts than fillies and usually first noticed when the animal is under 2 years old. Typically the affected horse loses normal control of its hind legs, which become inco-ordinated. This is most marked if the animal is trotted fast and then brought to a sudden halt, when it will sway and almost fall over behind. Most wobblers are incapable of backing or turning in a tight circle.

This condition never gets any better. Severely affected wobblers should therefore be destroyed, as they are all unsafe to ride.

Horses sometimes become wobblers as the result of an accident, such as rearing and falling over backwards, or getting cast in their boxes.

The condition is due to changes in the spinal column affecting the cord, which in turn produces inco-ordination in the hind-quarters.

Reference and further reading
Rossdale and Ricketts, *Equine Stud Medicine* Ballière and Tindall (London) (see pages 194 – 318).

SYMPTOMS GUIDE

Opposite is a quick guide to the symptoms of the various conditions which can affect young foals.

Symptom	Condition or disease	Reference Page
Above-normal temperature	Barkers and dummy foals	18
	Influenza	24
	Joint ill/navel ill	24
	Meningitis	26
	Nephritis	—
	Pneumonia	26
	Salmonella	29
	Scouring	19
	Septicaemia	29
	Strangles	30
	Swamp fever	20
Rapid breathing/respiratory distress	Barkers and dummy foals	18
	Haemolytic foals	22
	Influenza	24
	Joint ill/navel ill	24
	Meningitis	26
	Pneumonia	26
	Ruptured bladder	28
	Salmonella	29
	Septicaemia	29
	Strangles	30
Foal off suck (Loss of suck reflex or ability/inclination to nurse)	Barkers and dummy foals	18
	Haemolytic foals	22
	Joint ill/navel ill	24
	Meconium retention	25
	Meningitis	26
	Pneumonia	26
	Ruptured bladder	28
	Salmonella	29
	Septicaemia	29
	Sleepy foal disease	30
	Strangles	30
Scouring	Diarrhoea (general)	19
	Salmonella infection	29
	Septicaemia	29
	Worms	59
Blindness	Barkers and dummy foals	18
	Meningitis	26
Convulsions	Barkers and dummy foals	18
	Hepatitis	—
	Meningitis	26
Abnormal restlessness	Barkers	18

Symptom	Condition or disease	Reference Page
Yawning	Haemolytic foals	22
Dullness/Sleepiness	Haemolytic foals	22
	Nephritis	—
	Sleepy foal disease	30
Anaemia/Jaundice	Haemolytic foals	22
	Swamp fever	20
Difficulty in standing	Barkers and dummy foals	18
	Deformed limbs	33
	Haemolytic foals	22
	Joint ill	24
	Meningitis	26
	Shaker foals	30
	Weak limbs	32
Lying in awkward positions	Meconium colic	25
	Ruptured bladder	28
Straining	Meconium colic	25
	Ruptured bladder	28
Shivering	Pneumonia	26
	Shaker foals	30
Colic	Meconium colic	25
	Ruptured bladder	28
	Salmonella	29
	Worms	59
Watery eye	Entropion	20
Urine from navel/wet navel cord stump	Pervious urachus	26
Distended stomach	Ruptured bladder	28
	Meconium colic	25
	Scouring	19
Swelling in region of navel	Navel ill	24
	Hernia	23
Lameness	Bruised sole	—
	Joint ill	24
	Round joints	27
	Tetanus	31
	Wobblers	34
Inco-ordination of limbs	Wobblers	34
Swollen joints	Joint ill	24
	Round joints	27

Symptom	Condition or disease Reference	Page
Swellings in the angle of the jaw	Gutteral pouch tympanitis	21
	Herpes virus respiratory infection	27
	Snotty Noses	30
	Strangles	30
Nasal discharge	Herpes virus respiratory infection	27
	Influenza	24
	Pneumonia	26
	Snotty noses	30
Cough	Influenza	24
	Snotty noses	30
	Strangles	30
Regurgitating milk	Cleft palate	—
Dehydration (sunken eyeballs)	Diarrhoea (general)	19
	Peritonitis	—
	Salmonella infection	29

Characteristic abnormal lying positions of a foal with meconium colic.

CHAPTER FOUR

The importance of correct hoof care

Y OUNG HORSES MAY be ruined if their feet are neglected. In order to remain sound, win prizes at shows and obtain their full market value at sales, horses must have good conformation and move correctly. The shape and angle of the feet influences the way a foal's or yearling's legs develop. Foals which were normal at birth may have faulty limb conformation by the time they are 2 years old if their feet are neglected. Once the growth points in the legs have closed — normally by 2 years of age, no further correction is possible. Prevention calls for extreme vigilance on the part of the owner or stud groom, since faults can develop from one week to the next and due to the young horse's rapid growth rate may be fully established before the blacksmith's next visit.

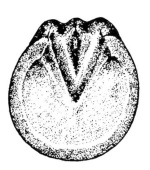

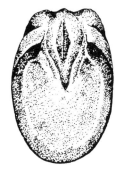

Fɪɢ 10 Normal foot

Contracted Foot
Watch out for this at all times but espcecially if the heels are left long for any reason.

The normal front foot is rounded at the toe. The inner quarter is slightly more upright than the outer and the angle of the foot at the toe should be approximately 45°; a lesser angle is found in sloping and flat feet, a greater one in upright, boxy or club feet.

Normal action is straight. When the horse is walking towards you the legs and feet should move in alignment with the body, the toe meeting the ground first and the foot being set down flat and evenly.

Uneven trimming or wear can turn a normal foot into an abnormal one and affects the horse's action. An upright foot develops when the heel is too high or too much hoof has been removed from the toe. This can be caused by incorrect rasping, continual pawing at the stable floor or hard ground, or as the result of a horse breaking off a piece of hoof at the toe. All these can have the effect of straightening the pastern and throwing the knee forward. A straight pastern may be associated with knuckling over at the fetlock joint which is also a symptom of epiphysitis in foals.

Where the horse is wearing away its feet by scraping at the floor, the effect is gradual and more likely to go unnoticed; therefore the habit is potentially dangerous. Examine the feet every day. As soon as any deviation is noticed, rasp the foot to restore a 45° angle at the toe. Where the cause cannot be removed or too

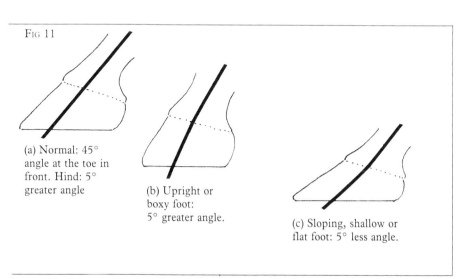

FIG 11

(a) Normal: 45° angle at the toe in front. Hind: 5° greater angle

(b) Upright or boxy foot: 5° greater angle.

(c) Sloping, shallow or flat foot: 5° less angle.

much hoof has been removed, light tips should be fitted to both front feet. These afford maximum frog pressure and encourage normal foot development. However, tips should only be fitted as a last resort since young horses turned out together are more likely to damage one another if they are shod.

Loose-boxes used for weaned foals and yearlings should be bedded down as deeply as possible, especially round the manger, walls and door area. This prevents injury and uneven foot wear due to scraping. For this reason peat moss deep litter is preferred for foals and yearlings.

A long foot is caused by excessive growth of horn at the toe or by overlowering the heels. It gives more slope to the pastern but also throws the knee back. It affords maximum frog pressure allowing the hoof to develop, but may predispose to stumbling and put strain on the knee joint and flexor tendons. Sometimes young horses have more natural slope on one pastern than the other. In these cases the heels should be trimmed to maintain an even slope and correct alignment of both legs. Foals and yearlings in weak condition often appear to have long sloping pasterns. In most cases these will come up as the horse gets stronger, but judicious trimming helps. It may not affect a horse's speed if he turns his feet in or out but it will affect his market value or show ring career, and may affect his long-term soundness.

Toes turned out is probably the most common abnormality seen in foals and yearlings. This too may be caused by weakness but if left uncorrected it may lead to a permanent deviation of the whole leg in later life. When the foot is turned out the hoof is not set down flat and evenly but instead lands on the inside toe causing greater wear to this side. The defect is often associated with brushing since the hoof tends to move inwards and then outwards as it travels forwards. Knocks commonly lead to the formation of splints. Splints may also occur in young horses which turn their feet out because strain is placed on the inside of the leg; the ligament binding the splint bone to the cannon bone is torn away from its attachment and new bone (a splint) is formed at the point of injury.

To correct a toes out position the outside wall should be lowered to level the foot. If this is not sufficient light shoes flattened at the toe to give more slip and built up on the inside

40

should be fitted and the horse walked on firm ground each day — for instance, round a concrete yard.

Conversely, when the foot turns in the hoof lands on the outside toe causing greater wear to this side. The defect is often associated with 'dishing' since the hoof tends to move outwards and then inwards as it travels forwards. Pigeon toes (turned in) may be associated with soreness somewhere on the inside of the leg. This causes the horse to walk with more weight on the outside of the hoof, to save the affected area. The extra wear to the outer wall pushes the toe in. Hence, when a splint is developing a perfectly straight action may suddenly become toes-in. Pigeon toes are also a characteristic of epiphysitis (inflammation of the growth points) immediately above the knee joint. Although this type of inflammation can occur on the outer aspect of the knee, it is more commonly seen on the inside. The pain or discomfort produced causes the horse to put more weight on the outer walls of the hooves, which soon wear down causing a toes-in position. Therefore, always look for a reason when correcting this fault.

To rectify a toes-in position the inside wall should be lowered to level the foot. If shoes are used they should be built up on the outside and the horse walked on firm ground each day.

Since young horses tend to spend long periods of their lives at grass, their feet are sometimes neglected between monthly visits by the blacksmith. The daily routine should include hoof inspection, this being the only way that faults can be spotted before they become established. Not only should the horses' feet be inspected for correct alignment but to avoid the occurrence of odd feet, the width of each foot, should be checked regularly for equal development.

CHAPTER FIVE

Weaning

IDEALLY ALL FOALS should remain with their mothers until they are at least 6 months old and have developed a full adult digestion.

Weaning is the process of separating the mare and foal when the foal is old enough to thrive on a solid diet alone. The very earliest age at which this can take place is when the foal is 4 months old, the optimum time for the average mare and foal to be weaned being at 6 months. There is however no definite time at which weaning should occur and it will depend largely on the general condition and health of the mare, i.e. pregnant or barren, and the health and maturity of the foal. For example if the mare is in-foal again, even though she may be fat it would be far better, in the interest of the foetus she is carrying, to wean her present foal at 6 months. In the case of an in-foal mare in poor condition, it might be advisable to wean the foal early at 4 months. The period between weaning and the last 3 months of pregnancy can be regarded as the 'rest period'. Fat barren mares, on the other hand, can be left with their foals until the following spring should the owner so desire. Mares usually produce their best foals the year after being barren.

If the foal at foot is weak or ill, it should not be weaned until it has recovered, as the act of weaning is always a shock to the foal's system, although the degree of stress depends to some extent on the method used. In cases where a sick foal goes 'off suck', the mare must be milked right out at least six times a day, to keep her in milk until the foal has recovered and starts sucking normally again. If this is not done the mare will cease to give milk, and the foal will be weaned prematurely.

Foals must be prepared for weaning if a major set-back is to be avoided. This means they must be introduced to the exact solid diet they are going to receive after weaning, some 3–4 weeks beforehand. Then they will be eating their total daily ration by weaning time. This is most important, otherwise the weaned foal will loose condition rapidly during the first few weeks of separation. The easiest way to get the foal to eat solid food is to feed the mare and foal at the same time, spreading the food out along a trough or manger. If necessary tie the mare up, so that she cannot bully the foal. The latter will soon learn by imitation and develop a liking for the food.

As foals get older they tend to spend less and less time close to their mothers and more time playing with the other foals in their group. They will establish friendships between themselves and this factor can be utilised to advantage for weaning.

Basically there are three methods of weaning foals:

(1) Paddock weaning

This method has the advantage that it can be used for a group of foals of different ages. Wherever possible this is the method of choice, as it produces less stress when compared with other methods. Also the foals need not be stabled but can be left out day and night if preferred.

Prior to weaning, the mares and foals are collected together into the same paddock so that the foals can get to know one another and become accustomed to their surroundings. At least 2 weeks should be allowed for this. It does not matter whether the mares and foals are stabled at night or if they are running out all the time. Before weaning starts check all the fences, making quite certain that they are stock proof. Select a second well-fenced paddock or field, for the mares after weaning, which is out of ear-shot of the foals' paddock.

Weaning should always take place in the morning on days when there are people available to keep an eye on both the newly weaned foals and the mares. Before weaning the foals, a plan of campaign must be worked out. Any vicious or restless mares should be removed first. On the first day two mares should be taken out so that they can be turned together into their selected paddock. After this the mares should be removed one at a time, the quietest and most gentle being left to last. No more than two mares should be weaned at the same time under this system.

On the selected morning, if the mares and foals are running out at grass all the time, the two mares to be removed are caught up and led off to their distant paddock, and the weaned foals left behind with their friends. If on the other hand the mares and foals are stabled at night, then the mares and foals are turned out as usual, the two foals to be weaned being left to last. They are led out of their boxes and up to the paddock gate as usual, but at this point the foals are taken into the paddock to join their friends and the mares are led away. The foals should not be loosed until the mares are out of sight. A third person should accompany the mares, to ensure that they walk on. Both the mares and foals should be watched until they have settled.

The two weaned foals will normally gallop up and down the fence a few times before joining their friends as usual. They never go to any of the mares and normally settle within an hour or two. In about 5 days another mare can be removed and so on until only one mare remains. The last mare can be left with the weaned foals for several weeks if so desired or she can be removed after a few days. Alternatively all the mares may be removed at the same time. The foals are left in their usual paddock and held until the mares are out of sight.

It is better not to put too large a group of mares and foals together for weaning. About ten mares is the maximum number for ease of operation, although no real danger is likely to occur if the number is greater.

Where the mares and foals are stabled at night the weaned foals should be brought in as usual and they *must be put back into their usual loose-boxes,* so there is the minimum of change in their daily routine.

The mares will not require any special treatment after weaning. Unless the weather is very wet and cold, they should be left out in their paddock day and night — this will help them to walk off the excess milk in their udders. If they are brought in at night they should only receive hay and water to encourage them to dry up quickly. On no account should any milk be drawn off, as this will only lead to more being produced, delay drying-up, and is a known cause of mastitis. Nature works on a supply-and-demand basis. If the demand for milk ceases then the supply also ceases.

Signs of mastitis in mares are usually a hot swollen udder with swellings extending forward along the underside of the belly and between the hind legs. The affected mare will usually walk stiffly and often go off her feed. If a little milk is drawn from the udder it will be thick and lumpy. Your veterinary surgeon should be consulted as he may wish to prescribe antibiotic treatment. Untreated mastitis can result in the loss of function of the affected parts of the udder.

(2) The traditional method

Under this system the weaned foal is put into a roomy loose-box and the mare is turned out into a well-fenced paddock out of earshot of her foal as described in paddock weaning.

The loose-box used for the foal should be large enough to allow it to have some exercise. The water bucket should be placed off the ground and hay nets should not be used. If replaced at a later date they should be tied up as high as possible, as young horses tend to play and can easily get a foot caught in a loose hay-net. The manger system as described on page 52 is probably the safest and most practical for all horses.

Plenty of bedding should be put in the loose-box to prevent injury. The droppings should be picked up each day, but it will not be necessary to muck out the box completely.

As weaning usually takes place in the late summer or early autumn when the weather may be hot, a wire cage should be fitted over the top door of the loose-box so that the foal can get plenty of air and ventilation without being able to jump out. If your loose-box is not fitted with a wire cage, one can be improvised quite simply by making a wooden frame the same size as the top door of the loose-box and nailing some ½ inch (1.25cm) wire netting over the frame. This can then be tied in place with string to the hinges and fittings of the top door.

On no account should foals be shut away in darkened loose-boxes at weaning. Some people shut the top doors of the foals' loose-boxes and cover the windows up, maintaining that the foals settle down better if they are kept in semi-darkness. This is probably the finest way of encouraging foals to develop such bad habits as crib-biting and weaving, and is not recommended.

45

On the day selected for weaning bring the mare and foal in from the paddock and put them in the prepared loose-box. Put a bridle on the mare. With the help of at least one person, walk the mare out of the box, leaving the foal alone inside and shut *both* the top and bottom doors. Make sure someone is walking behind the mare to prevent her from stopping or trying to run back to her foal as you take her to the paddock.

Several mares can be weaned together and turned out into the paddock at the same time. If only one mare is to be weaned then a suitably quiet companion must be found to run with her, at least for the first week or so until she has settled down.

Turn the weaned mares loose in the paddock and stand by the gate until they settle and start to graze peacefully, which may take an hour or more. Once the mares have settled it is quite all right to return to the yard and see to the weaned foals. If it is a hot day the top doors of the loose-boxes should be left open with the wire cages in place. The foals can be given a feed — this *must be exactly the same ration they received before weaning.*

After about 2 – 3 days the foals can be turned out for exercise into a well-fenced paddock where they can easily be observed. If only one foal has been weaned a very quiet companion, preferably of about the same size, should be found to run with the foal. If no such companion is available, then the foal should only be turned out for short periods at a time, when it can be watched carefully. Foals are completely without fear or any knowledge of their own capabilities. This can prove lethal at times, as they will often take on fences, hedges or gates which would stop any normal self-respecting adult horse.

Weaned foals should be brought in at night for at least 2 – 3 weeks after weaning. If you decide to turn them out again a dry warm period must be chosen for the first nights out, otherwise the young horses could feel cold and wet and under these stress conditions develop any infection which happened to be around.

(3) Weaning by pairs

Some people prefer to wean two foals at a time and put them together in the same loose-box. This method has the advantage that foals tend to settle down more quickly than they do under the traditional method. However it does entail a further period of weaning at a later date when the two foals have to be separated. Another disadvantage is that one foal is almost certainly going to be the 'boss', so unless the food is supplied *ad lib,* or a constant watch kept at feeding time, one is bound to eat more than the other.

Another method used on some studs is to put a metal grille in the dividing walls of the loose-boxes, so that the horses can see their neighbours.

When horses are left entirely to nature, weaning normally takes place when the foal is about a year old, shortly before the next foal is born. This is not practical where horses are being bred commercially for showing or the sales. In these cases the foals need to be separated from their mothers so that they can be handled and fed in preparation for their future role in life, and for the shows or sales in which they are to be entered.

Some colt foals will mount their mothers as early as 1 month old, however they are not capable of getting a mare in foal until they are about 16 months old, but they should be separated from the filly foals at about 9 months, as their play is so much rougher than the fillies' that accidents can happen.

CHAPTER SIX

Feeding youngstock

How a young horse is fed from birth to maturity affects its constitution and soundness. Injudicious feeding can produce conditions identical in character to inherited defects. It is therefore sometimes difficult to differentiate between inherited and environmentally produced abnormalities. For instance epiphysitis (inflammation of the growth points in foals and yearlings) can be due to over-feeding or an imbalance in the calcium: phosphorus ratio, as well as trauma or an inherited weakness.

Growth rate is most rapid from birth to 3½ months with an average gain of 3lb (1.4kg) daily,[*] falling to only 1.2lb (0.5kg) per day between 7 and 18 months old. Dietary errors are more readily exposed when growth rate exceeds the normal. Slower growth rates make less demand on the diet. An even growth rate which is close to optimum for the breed or type should therefore be maintained. Guard against periods of rapid growth such as those which can occur after a set-back. A sudden surge in weight gain[†] predisposes to such conditions as upright pasterns and knuckling over at the fetlock joints in foals and yearling. Over-feeding young horses before their limb epiphyses have closed is a known cause of epiphysitis.

Digestion of fibre is not fully effective until the foal reaches 6 to 7 months old. The foal's ability to digest hay gradually improves over this 7-month period. Therefore, hay used for foals must be of the very highest quality, with plenty of leaf and not stalky. The ability to digest sucrose also develops over the same period. At

[*] Breuer L. H. Proc. Md. Nutr. Conf. p.102 (1974).
[†] Hintz H. F., H. F. Schryver and J. E. Lowe, Proc. Cornell Nutr. Conf., p.94 (1976).

birth it is considered to be 30 per cent efficient, at 4 months 40 per cent efficient, and 100 per cent efficient by 7 months of age. Young foals should therefore not receive foods such as molassed sugar beet pulp, which contain sucrose.

From birth young foals* should be allowed free access to the food manger with their dams. Mare's milk does not contain sufficient nutrients (protein, energy, calcium or phosphorus) to supply all the foal's needs after the first week. It must, therefore, receive an additional ration each day. Since the mare also requires concentrates in order to milk well, the foal can be encouraged to share its mother's food or, if preferred, use a creep feeder.

A sample creep ration might consist of:

	Percentage of ration
Oats, crushed or rolled	72.75
Barley, cooked	5.00
Heat treated full-fat soya bean meal	15.00
Dried skimmed milk powder	5.00
Calcium lactate	0.75
Vitamin/mineral supplement	1.5

A vitamin pre-mix for foals and youngstock up to a year old should contain vitamins A, D_3, E, K, dried yeast (which will supply most of the B vitamins) and B_{12}.

The following essential minerals should be included in all horse rations: calcium, phosphorus, sodium, chlorine; also the trace elements: copper, iron, iodine, manganese, zinc and selenium. Cobalt is not needed if B_{12} is included in the vitamin pre-mix. Similarly, if the protein quality of the ration is high, the addition of sulphur will be unnecessary. Magnesium in grass may be less available at certain times of the year so is included as a preautionary measure. Potassium is necessary for animals in work.

Vitamin and mineral pre-mixes must be made up by chemists for horse owners and not by the stables themselves. Poor mixing or inaccurate measuring could result in toxic levels being fed to stock.

---

*Leighton Hardman A. C., *Equine Nutrition,* 8, 88, Pelham Books (1980).

Most of the feeds used in horse rations are higher in phosphorus than calcium. Since horses require more dietary calcium than phosphorus, calcium must be added. The following calcium: phosphorus ratios are recommended:

	Calcium:phosphorus ratio (D.M. Basis)
Foals	1.5 : 1
Yearlings	1.7 : 1
Two-and three-year-olds	2.0 : 1

The calcium and/or phosphorus supplements most commonly used in horse rations are:

Ground limestone (calcium carbonate)
Dicalcium phosphate
Calcium lactate
Calcium gluconate
Steamed bone flour

All foods contain protein. Proteins are made up from amino acids. The levels and combinations of these amino acids make each food different from the rest. Young horses up to 2 years old, broodmares and horses in hard work require diets which supply sufficiently high levels of the essential amino acids to cover their needs. Those foodstuffs which are high in the essential amino acids are known as 'quality' proteins. They are used in the diet to balance the amino-acid deficiency of the cereal grains, which are 'poor quality' proteins.

The 'quality' protein feeds commonly used to balance horse rations are:

Extracted or full-fat soya bean meal
High-grade, white fish meal
Dried skimmed milk powder

During digestion nitrogen is removed from any excess dietary protein. The residue serves as an additional source of energy or is stored as fat.

Poor quality protein diets affect energy utilisation. If the amino acid/calorie ratio of the diet is too low, less dietary energy is utilised and more food is required to achieve normal growth rate and performance. As the energy content of the ration increases so the amino-acid requirement increases. The better balanced the diet is, the more efficient energy utilisation becomes and the less food is needed to achieve the same results.

The young horse's protein requirement is given as:*

	Total diet % crude protein (D.M. basis)
Foals up to weaning (6 months)	18 – 16
Foals (6 – 12 months)	16 – 13.5
Yearlings and 2-year-olds	13.5 – 11
Youngstock 3 years and over (idle)	10

The poorer the quality of the hay or pasture used the higher must be the quality of the concentrate ration in order to balance the deficiency.

Vitamin B_{12} is required for protein utilisation. Providing there is an adequate level of this vitamin in the ration, no adverse effects will occur if there is a modest excess of protein in the diet.

Youngstock consume an average 3 per cent of their body weight in food per day. Therefore their requirement for nutrients must be met within the bounds of this 3 per cent limit. The ratio of hay or grass to concentrate mix gradually increases as the young horse gets older. Weaned foals receive approximately 70 per cent mix to 30 per cent hay but by the time they are 2 years old the ratio is usually 60 per cent hay to 40 per cent mix.

A sample ration for weaned foals and youngstock might consist of:

	Percentage of ration
Oats (bruised or crushed)	70.75
Barley (cooked)	5.0
Extracted or full-fat soya bean meal	15.0
Dehydrated lucerne alfalfa meal (18 per cent protein grade)	7.0

*Nutrient Requirements of the Horse, N.R.C., Washington, 6 p.33. (1978).

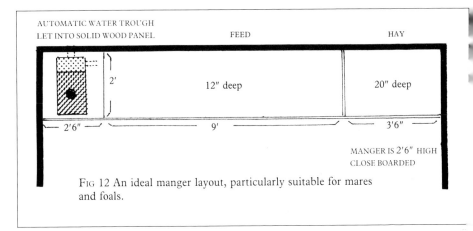

AUTOMATIC WATER TROUGH
LET INTO SOLID WOOD PANEL   FEED   HAY

2'   12" deep   20" deep

2'6"   9'   3'6"

MANGER IS 2'6" HIGH
CLOSE BOARDED

Fig 12 An ideal manger layout, particularly suitable for mares and foals.

Calcium lactate   0.75
Vitamin/mineral supplement   1.5

Bran is not recommended as a feed for youngstock. Although it traditionally accompanies oats, other foods such as dried lucerne (alfalfa) give better results. Samples of bran may contain 17% crude protein, however, the value of the protein is low. Bran also contains high levels of phosphorus (0.84 per cent) and low levels of calcium (0.16 per cent). Diets containing high levels of bran have been known to produce such conditions as obscure lameness, splints and enlargements of the jaw and face. This is due to excess phosphorus coupled with low levels of available calcium.

Several studies in the U.S.A. indicate that dried lucerne (alfalfa) is an excellent feed for horses. It gives a physiological response in excess of its food value and is therefore thought to contain an un-identified factor. Foals from mares receiving dehydrated alfalfa[*] were much above average in physical condition with no contracted tendons or crooked legs. The calcium content is high − 1.44 per cent − with phosphorus only 0.22 per cent; it therefore helps to balance other ingredients in the ration, such as oats, barley, soya bean meal and linseed. Dried lucerne should be fed to youngstock in place of bran in the diet. 8 m.m. cubes are preferred for horses, as they do not need to be soaked before feeding.

[*]Bailey J.H. *Feedstuffs 42*, 22, (1970)

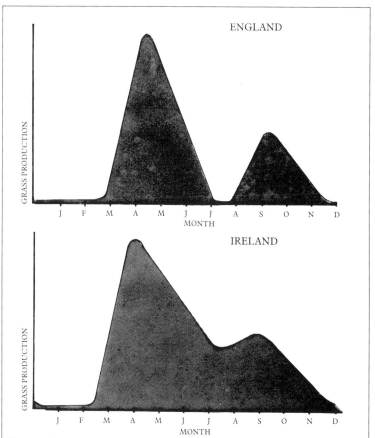

ENGLAND

IRELAND

FIG 13 Graph showing average annual grass production for England and Ireland. The low trough between July and August is due to drought periods – more often seen in eastern areas of the U.K. Horses' diets must be supplemented when grass production falls below the horses' requirement.

Polyunsaturated fats are used extensively to produce healthy skins and coats in show stock. Fat supplies 2.25 times as many calories as carbohydrate. Fats and oils can therefore be used as a rich source of energy for animals in hard work. Care should be taken when adding high calorie foods to the diet of other young horses.* The level of oil normally added is between 2 and 5 per

* Cunha A.G., *Horse feeding and Nutrition*, 9, p.134, Academic Press (1980).

cent of the total ration. Those generally used arc:

> Cod liver oil
> Linseed oil (animal feed grade)
> Vegetable oil (corn or sunflower seed)
> (or by feeding full fat soya bean meal)

Cod liver oil has the advantage that it also contains vitamins A and D. Vitamin D is essential for the proper absorption of dietary calcium and phosphorus.

Since the unsaturated fats are highly susceptible to rancidity, unless anti-oxidants have been used in their preparation, care must be taken. Heat, moisture and light accelerate rancidity which in turn destroys vitamin A, carotene, vitamin E, biotin and other nutrients. Feeding rancid oil (or grain which has been allowed to go rancid) can, therefore, predispose horses to such conditions as 'tying-up'. Oil should be bought in small quantities and stored in a cool, dark place.

Heat treated, full fat (unextracted) soya bean meal may be used to replace extracted soya bean meal in the diet of young horses, especially before shows and sales.

CHAPTER SEVEN

The management of weaned foals

Due to the cost of keeping horses these days, people are no longer prepared to give high prices for animals which are not absolutely sound, well grown and of good conformation. Also, as far as pedigree stock are concerned, they must be well bred. For anything less there is little or no demand. In the face of such a selective market the production of saleable young horses has become more of an exact science than ever before, and attention to detail the most important single factor.

Failing the personal approach good enthusiastic staff is an essential factor for success. Otherwise the commercial production of young horses is better not attempted these days. This means that an interest in the stock must be cultivated, usually by means of bonuses on sales and show-ring successes.

With the removal of their mothers weaned foals will usually relate more to the humans who look after them and so become easier to manage. It is essential that weaned foals are handled every day during the winter period, as their contact with humans will be less once they are turned out to grass in the spring.

Most horses will learn words of command in much the same way as a dog. At this stage the foal should be introduced to such words as WALK ON, WHOA and BACK. The less words you use for any command the simpler it is for the foal to understand. WALK ON should be made to sound energetic, while WHOA is long-drawn-out and soothing. BACK should be taught while standing directly in front of the foal and pushing it back one or two strides. These first lessons are the foundation for future schooling.

To catch a nervous foal, always approach it quietly and move your hand slowly. Never attempt to grab the headcollar but gradually move your hand under its muzzle, palm uppermost; wait for it to drop its head to examine your hand, then slowly get hold of the back of the headcollar noseband.

In order to lead your foal safely, the rein should never be attached to the headcollar. Ask your saddler to cut a length of tubular web lungeing rein about 10 feet (3m) long. Ask him to turn the cut ends inside the web before stitching. This way the rein will be smooth and therefore easily pull free from the headcollar when necessary. The rein is passed through the back of the headcollar noseband evenly to form a leading rein. Should the young horse ever get away from you the rein will drop from the headcollar within the space of a few strides. There are many cases on record where horses have been killed by running away in panic at the sight and feel of a loose rein trailing round their legs.

At least once a week walk the foal out on a flat, hard surface to check that it is moving straight. Stand it on level ground to see that the angles of the front legs and feet are normal or improving. Rasp the feet as necesary but remember that any correction must be made gradually. Sudden alterations to the bearing surface of the foot put excessive strain on the joints. Examine the legs for signs of epiphysitis, splints, curbs etc. Check the fetlocks of foals under a year old, and the knees of foals or yearlings for signs of warmth – an early sign of developing epiphysitis.

Pick the foals' feet out daily and check that their feet are developing evenly in size. By handling their feet and legs regularly they will become very quiet for the blacksmith to handle and so enable him to trim their feet in the middle of the paddock during the summer. Examine daily for injuries.

Foals' mouths should be examined regularly to ensure that the incisors are in contact and developing normally. Many foals' teeth are over-shot but still in contact at weaning time; most will be fully in contact by the time they are yearlings. A few foals are born parrot-mouthed – that is, the lower incisors do not make contact with the upper incisors but slide up behind them to the roof of the mouth. In these cases some authorities recommend filing the teeth right back to encourage contact and normal development.

A colt's testicles can usually be felt at weaning time but there is no need to panic yet if only one can be found. By the time the colt is a year old both should be clearly visible and will tend to develop with exercise. Some colts do not drop their second testicle until they are 2 years old, so cannot be designated rigs until this age.

Manes and tails should be kept in perfect condition. Foals' manes initially grow in an upward direction but by the time they are old enough to be weaned, their manes should be lying on the off-side of the neck. This is encouraged by brushing the hair over with a damp body brush each day.

Young horses running out at grass together often develop the habit of chewing manes and tails. This results in a 'crew cut' effect, spoiling the appearance of any horse. Manes and tails must be examined daily for signs of chewing. The most effective deterrents are Cribox and Renardine. The former can be obtained from most saddlers and the latter from hardware stores. Mix Renardine with cooking oil – use an old bucket and keep it especially for this purpose. Wearing rubber gloves, apply the mixture to the manes and tails twice a week or more often if necessary. Cribox should be applied neat. Both will wash out using an animal shampoo.

Some young horses rub their manes and tails. The cause of rubbing must be established before treatment is commenced. It is usually due to one of three problems:

> (1) The effect of worms, in particular the seat worm (*oxyuris equi*). The female lays her eggs around the anus, setting up an irritation which causes the horse to rub these parts.

> (2) The presence of lice or mites in the mane and tail, in which case an application of louse powder benzyl benzoate or tetmosol, applied undiluted daily to the affected areas, will usually cure the condition.

> (3) Some horses, particularly ponies, are allergic to certain flies which are prevalent during the summer months. The resulting allergy causes the animal to rub its mane and tail, often until they are raw. The condition is known as 'Sweet Itch'. Affected animals must be brought inside for an hour before sunset – the time when this species of fly is most active. Stables should be equipped with an effective fly-killing device.

Yearlings of both sexes may be allowed to run together at grass until January or early February at the latest. After this the sexes must be separated. As they get older, so the colts' play becomes rougher and they will start to knock the fillies about. Once they reach puberty (at approximately 16 months old) they should not be placed in paddocks adjoining those containing fillies or mares.

During their first winter the leg epiphyses of young horses are still open and therefore susceptible to the effects of standing for prolonged periods on hard floors. Since foals and yearlings are normally turned out between the hours of 8.0 a.m. and 4.0 p.m during the winter, they spend some 16 hours in their loose-boxes.

Straw bedding does not entirely cushion the effect of a hard floor, so it is suggested that peat moss deep litter is a better form of bedding for all weaned foals and yearlings, producing fewer leg problems.

Animals which are to be sold as foals must have their manes pulled and should be presented at the sales bitted. Nylon or rubber bits are normally used at this stage. Small in-hand bridles may be worn or the bit attached to a smart headcollar (see chapter 9).

It is unnecessary to walk foals for longer than half an hour, twice a day, before the sales.

58

CHAPTER EIGHT

Parasites

Internal parasites

Worms are parasites. A parasite is an organism which lives on or in another organism (in this case the horse) deriving its nourishment from the host animal without actually killing it. If the parasite does destroy its host it is defeating its own object by depriving itself of a place to live and reproduce its species. Therefore where an animal dies as a direct result of a worm infestation it is a grave error on the part of the worms and not the inevitable result in a natural course of events.

Why then should we worry too much about worm parasites? The reason is that horses which have not previously come in contact with worm infections are not immune to their effects — while other immune but infected horses are capable of infecting all other horses with which they are turned out. The external signs of parasitism are:

(i) Loss of weight
(ii) Loss of condition, poor coat
(iii) Debility
(iv) Anaemia
(v) Colic
(vi) Death

At all costs one should avoid letting paddocks become infested with worm parasites. Adult horses will show signs of infection especially from *strongylus vulgaris*. Youngstock are badly affected by all species of worm parasite and despite good feeding will always look poor and stunted. They will consume as much if not more food than uninfected animals, but have a very low food conversion ratio, which will result in poor condition and stunted

59

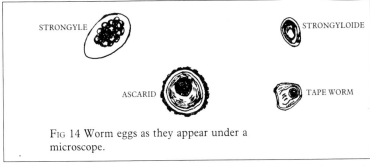

Fig 14 Worm eggs as they appear under a microscope.

growth but with normal costs of production. After worming, such stock may show signs of epiphysitis.*

The worm parasites usually involved are:

(i) Red worms, large and small
(ii) Round worms
(iii) Strongyloides
(iv) Tapeworms
(v) Seat worms
(vi) Lungworms
(vii) Liver fluke
(viii) Bots.

A complete list of these worms and their various degrees of pathogenicity is given opposite:

The strongyles are by far the most common and important species and this is the family of the large red worm. The adults live in the intestines, where the females lay their eggs, which pass out in the droppings on to the grass. They hatch out into larvae and climb up the blades of grass, where they hope to be eaten by their particular host animal. Any larvae which are fortunate enough to be eaten pass with the grass into the animal's stomach. If the animal is their particular host species they will survive; if not, they are destroyed. Larvae which survive migrate through the intestinal walls, travelling up the mesenteric arteries; that is, except for the small strongyle which remains in the walls of the intestines. The mature larvae eventually return to the intestines, become adults and the females commence egg laying.

* Hintz H.F., *et al*, Proc. Cornell Nutr. Conf., p.94 (1976).

Common internal parasites of the horse

Group	Common Name	Proper Name	Degree of Pathogenicity
1 (a)	Large red worms	*Strongylus vulgaris*	++++
		Strongylus equinus	++
		Strongylus edentatus	++
(b)	Small red worms	*Trichonema*	+
		Triodontophorus	+
		Trichostrongylus axei (common also to cattle and sheep)	+
(c)	Round worm	*Parascaris equorum*	+++
(d)	Strongyloides	*Strongyloides westeri*	+
(e)	Seat worm	*Oxyuris equi*	±
2	Tapeworm	*Anoplocephala pertoliata*	±
3	Lungworm	*Dictyocaulus arnfieldi*	++
4	Liver fluke	*Fasciola hepatica*	±
5	Bots	*Gastrophilus*	±

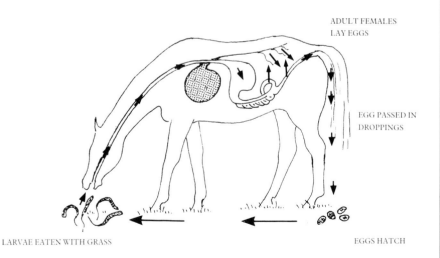

LARVAE MIGRATE THROUGH THE GUT WALL, INTO THE BLOOD VESSELS AND RETURN TO THE LARGE INTESTINE TO BECOME ADULTS.

ADULT FEMALES LAY EGGS

EGG PASSED IN DROPPINGS

LARVAE EATEN WITH GRASS

EGGS HATCH

Fig 15 The life cycle of the red worm

The complete cycle takes about 6 months. Migrating larvae can cause aneurisms to form at the root of the mesenteric arteries, which may result in the sudden death of the horse, or cause damage to part of the gut, which results in chronic intermittent colic.

The ascarid (round worm) is most commonly associated with foals and youngstock under 3 years old. These can be seen in the droppings of infected stock as they measure up to 14 inches (35cm) long. Large infestations of this worm can cause intestinal obstructions and perforation of the bowel, the latter resulting in a fatal peritonitis. Adult horses appear to have a high resistance to ascarid infection. The eggs are passed in the droppings on to the pasture in the same way as strongyle eggs but in this case they do not hatch but are eaten with the grass and develop inside the host animal — the life cycle of the round worm can be seen in Fig. 16. The complete life cycle takes about 60 days.

Strongyloides are common in young foals. They appear to be self-limiting, as they are seldom found in the droppings of older

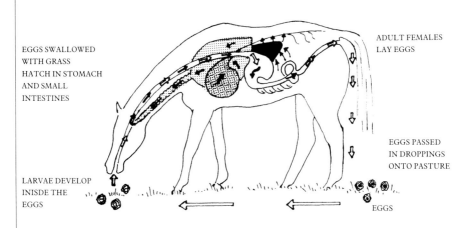

LARVE PASS FROM THE SMALL INTESTINE TO THE LIVER → FROM THE LIVER VIA THE BLOODSTREAM TO THE HEART AND LUNGS → PASS UP THE WIND-PIPE TO THE PHARYNX → SWALLOWED → RETURN TO THE STOMACH → FINALLY REACH THE LARGE INTESTINE WHERE THE FEMALES LAY EGGS.

ADULT FEMALES LAY EGGS

EGGS SWALLOWED WITH GRASS HATCH IN STOMACH AND SMALL INTESTINES

EGGS PASSED IN DROPPINGS ONTO PASTURE

LARVAE DEVELOP INISDE THE EGGS

EGGS

FIG 16 The life cycle of the round worm

animals; they are therefore of little consequence, although some authorities maintain that they can be responsible for scouring in foals.

The eggs of the seat worm (threadworm) are seldom, if ever, found in faeces samples sent for laboratory analysis, due to the fact that the female worm lays its eggs around the anus and not in the intestine like the previously described species of worm parasites. The eggs of the seat worm usually set up an irritation causing the horse to rub its tail and hind-quarters.

Tapeworms seldom cause much trouble in horses unless there is a large infestation.

Lungworms are most often found in the donkey, which appears to be their natural host, and seldom produce symptoms unless accompanied by a secondary infection. In the horse, however, they often produce symptoms of coughing and broken wind — even in the case of small infections. Where lungworm occurs in the horse it usually originates from an infected donkey.

The life cycle of the lungworm differs from those already mentioned in that although the female lays her eggs in the intestines, they hatch by the time they are passed in the droppings. The larvae mature on the pasture and are eaten with the grass. When consumed by the horse or donkey, they pass down into the intestines. From the intestines they enter the lymphatic system and so reach the right side of the heart. From the right ventricle they become blood-borne and migrate to the lungs; here they break out into the air passages and eventually reach the windpipe, when they are either coughed up and swallowed or pass up in the mucus and are swallowed, returning to the intestines where the females commence egg laying. The worm found in the horse is *Dictyocaulus arnfieldi* which, in common with most other equine worms, is specific and differs from those causing lungworm infections in other classes of farm stock.

Horses are sometimes infected by liver fluke, but only in areas where these parasites are found in other stock because the intermediary snail host is present.

Bots are normally not so much a problem in the British Isles and Ireland as they are in some other parts of the world. The bot fly attacks the horse by laying eggs on its forelegs, neck and mane,

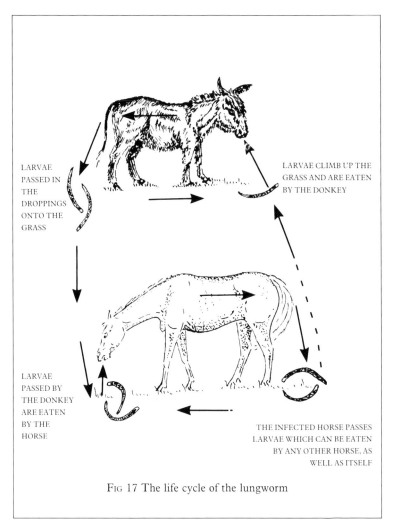

LARVAE PASSED IN THE DROPPINGS ONTO THE GRASS

LARVAE CLIMB UP THE GRASS AND ARE EATEN BY THE DONKEY

LARVAE PASSED BY THE DONKEY ARE EATEN BY THE HORSE

THE INFECTED HORSE PASSES LARVAE WHICH CAN BE EATEN BY ANY OTHER HORSE, AS WELL AS ITSELF

FIG 17 The life cycle of the lungworm

where the horses can lick them off easily. The eggs hatch into larvae in the horse's stomach and attach themselves to the walls where they remain for about 12 months. Large numbers of larvae can cause blockages, impaired digestion, colic and sometimes rupture of the stomach. To control infection, eggs should be removed from the horse's coat and larvae eliminated from the stomach by drugs recommended for the treatment of bots, such as Ivermectin (Eqvalan).

External parasites

Lice are often associated with worm infections in horses. They are more prevalent during warm wet winters than they are when the weather is really cold and frosty. Two distinct varieties are found on the horse: the biting louse and the sucking louse. Lice cause considerable irritation and affected horses will soon rub themselves raw in patches and lose condition rapidly. If the horse's coat is turned back, particularly in the areas of the mane and tail, lice can usually be seen with the naked eye.

Liberal dressings with louse powder, repeated at weekly intervals until all trace of lice have disappeared, are usually all that is required. Care should be taken not to get any louse powder in the animal's eyes as it will cause inflammation.

Ringworm is a highly contagious fungal skin disease of horses and cattle which is transmittable to humans. Care should therefore be taken when handling animals with this disease.

Affected horses will first be seen to have small slightly raised round spots from which, in a matter of a few days, the hair drops out, leaving small, round, bare patches — hence the name. These will increase in diameter if left untreated and become crusty.

If you suspect that a horse has ringworm, it should be isolated immediately and your veterinary surgeon consulted.

Horses, like cattle, can be attacked by warble flies, which lay their eggs on the horse's legs. The larvae hatch and burrow under the skin. As they mature they make their way towards the animal's back, where they eventually form small lumps each with a characteristic hole in the middle through which the larvae breath and through which they eventually hatch. Larvae should be removed surgically by your veterinary surgeon, before they have time to hatch.

Preventing internal parasites

Methods of preventing an internal parasitic problem on studs are:

(1) Regular dosing of all animals

All foals should be wormed against both strongyle and ascarid infections from the time they are 2 months old at regular 6 – 8 week intervals. Wormers are continually being improved, so consult your veterinary surgeon at least once a year for up to date information on available drugs.

The young horse's ability to thrive and grow normally depends on several factors, one of the most important being the drug and worming programme you choose.

Most wormers are now available as paste-filled syringes. The dose volume is normally set, according to the horse's weight,* by means of a 'twist-slide' adjustment ring on the plunger shaft.

The paste is deposited over the back of the horse's tongue. This eliminates the problem of some horses not eating up their food when a worm dose has been included.

Every horse on the stud must be included in the worming programme for it to be successful, even if it is only a retired hunter or pony. Animals running at grass must be caught up and wormed regularly every 6 – 8 weeks.

Worm parasites have the ability, in order to save themselves, of becoming immune to the effects of some drugs if these are used continuously for a long period of time. Therefore to be really effective the drug used may have to be changed from time to time. This will have the effect of not allowing the worms sufficient time to develop any immunity and so an effective programme of worm destruction is maintained.

Most authorities, at the moment, recommend the use of products containing ivermectin.

(2) Paddock management

Ideally all droppings should be removed from the paddocks daily, but with the present high cost of labour this is not always a practical proposition. However, every effort should be made to remove droppings from the smaller or most heavily used paddocks, otherwise they will tend to become 'horse-sick'.

From the point of view of worm control, paddocks should be rested for the 6 month winter period, when frost will drastically reduce the numbers of surviving larvae.

Horses are very selective in their grazing habits and will only graze areas which have not been contaminated by their own droppings; this is a limited natural safeguard against self-infection with worm parasites. Large areas of paddock will tend to be rejected by the horses with the result that unless the grass is kept

---

* For details of weight estimation formulae, see *Equine Nutrition*, p.18, A.C. Leighton Hardman, Pelham Books.

topped regularly it may grow very long and coarse in places. As an alternative to topping, a herd of de-horned or naturally polled cattle may be grazed with the horses. They are less selective in their grazing habits and will clear the areas of long grass left by the horses. Apart from *Trichostrongylus axei,* which is parasitic for cattle, sheep and horses, any worm larvae consumed by the cattle will be destroyed and so the number of worm larvae on the paddocks will be greatly reduced. Ideally one should maintain a grazing rate of one-fifth horses to cattle, but this is not always feasible. When selecting cattle for a stud farm it is important to choose a quiet breed such as the Simmental or Hereford.

The practice of harrowing paddocks to scatter the droppings only has the effect of contaminating larger areas and reducing the clean area available to the horses. In summary droppings should be removed from the paddocks at least once a week and the paddocks rested for a minimum of 3 consecutive months each year, or inter-grazed with cattle.

(3) Routine analysis of droppings samples*

Although horses may be wormed at regular intervals, it does not necessary mean that they are no longer passing any worm eggs in their droppings. Some worms manage to develop an immunity to a particular drug or drugs and will continue to survive despite treatment. Therefore a periodic check should be made to make sure that all animals are free from worms.

For faecal worm egg counts the samples must be as fresh as possible. They should be placed in an air-tight container, such as a sealed polythene bag. They must not be allowed to dry out and must be kept as cool as possible so that the eggs will not hatch before they can be counted. The sooner the samples are taken or sent to the laboratory for testing the better. Samples should be taken from the centre of droppings and should represent more than one pile of droppings from the same horse. They must be clearly marked (at the time of collection) with the horse's identity.

For a lungworm larvae count you will need to collect enough droppings to fill a ½lb (227gm) honey jar; half this quantity is sufficient for a standard worm egg count.

---

* For details of how to carry out a simple faecal egg count test see Chapter 16 of *Stallion Management,* A. C. Leighton Hardman, Pelham Books.

CHAPTER NINE

A guide to early education

I<small>F YOU HAVE</small> not had experience of handling horses, practise everything on an older horse until you are proficient, before attempting to handle or teach a young horse anything.

The more time you can devote to a young horse the better — never rush its education at any stage. The first essential is that young horses should walk out freely when led and never get away from you. Foals and yearlings should be mouthed therefore, long before they are strong enough to break free when being led from a headcollar. Once learnt, this is a difficult habit to cure and may result in injury one day.

In order to mouth a young horse you will need a flexible straight bar rubber snaffle, a straight bar metal bit with keys, and a bridle. The bit may be attached to the headcollar but a finer adjustment can be achieved if a bridle is used. Bit straps or clips are necessary with a headcollar, although baler twine can be equally effective. Straps are preferred to clips since the latter have been known to catch on the horse's lip.

For the first few lessons the bridle should be stripped down until only the headpiece and cheek straps remain. Select the rubber snaffle. It is normally easier to put a bit into the horse's mouth with as few people involved as possible. In other words, if one person can manage quietly, on his or her own, this is better than having two or three people around the horse at the same time.

If you are using a bridle, leave the headcollar and lead rein on, then pass the bridle slowly across the horse's neck and very slowly move it up to the correct position just behind the ears. Attach the rubber snaffle to the off-side cheek strap, but keep hold of the bit all the time. If the horse happened to toss its head it would almost certainly receive a blow to the side of its face from a loose bit. Move round to the near side, hold the bit in the flat of your left hand and insert your thumb gently into the corner of the mouth on this side and wriggle it if necessary. This will cause the jaw to relax. Slip the bit into the mouth, making sure you do not catch the teeth. Never try to force the bit between the horse's teeth. This will encourage it to throw its head up. Secure the near-side bit ring to the cheek strap. As the bridle has no browband it could slip back, and should therefore be tied to the headcollar.

When a headcollar is used in place of the bridle, attach the bit straps to the headcollar and then fasten them onto the bit rings.

If you prefer to use two people to put the bit in a young horse's mouth, they should take up positions one each side of the horse's head and hold the ring of the bit, headcollar or cheek strap nearest them. One should gently open the horse's mouth, as already described, and then the bit should be eased into place and attached to the bridle or headcollar on each side.

To encourage the development of a wet mouth the key bit should be used in place of the rubber bit as soon as the young horse is accepting the latter. The rubber bit is not reintroduced until the horse is led from the bit. Very strong or fresh horses may need to be led from a straight bar metal snaffle throughout their careers.

It is preferable to adjust the bit so that it just wrinkles the corners of a young horse's mouth. This lessens the chance of it getting its tongue over the bit, especially when playing with the keys.

Mouthing should be carried out in a loose-box, but first check that there are no nails or projections on which the rings of the bit

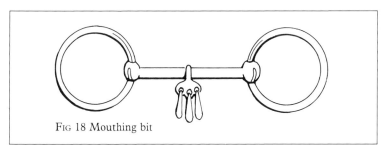

Fig 18 Mouthing bit

69

could get caught. If there is no cage over the door, the top door should be shut so that the horse cannot get itself hooked up on the door fastenings, and possibly break its neck.

Bit straps are safer than clips, as already stated, and straight bar mouthing bits are safer than similar jointed bits with keys. The latter have a central ring through which some horses manage to jam the keys and so bruise the roof of the mouth. When buying mouthing bits always check that both the keys and centre ring have been closed up tightly and are free from sharp edges. Stainless steel bits are worth the extra expense if youngstock are produced on an annual basis.

To remove the bridle without allowing the horse to develop the bad habit of tossing its head, stand by its near-side shoulder facing the front. Grasp the headpiece at its junction with the throat lash, the off-side in your right hand passed under the neck and the near-side in your left hand. Lift the bridle over the horse's ears. Initially the bridle should be dismantled in order to remove it, unbuckling the bit first. After the first week most horses can be introduced to the idea of the straps passing their eyes as the bridle is removed in one piece.

It usually takes a little longer before the bridle can be put on in one piece. No book can tell you the exact psychological moment when this can be done as it will vary with each individual. However, in the meantime the browband can be added. This must be long enough to hang loosely on the forehead and so avoid pressure on the back of the ears. At first it should be attached to the off-side of the bridle only, then passed across the forehead and slipped onto the near-side headpiece.

When putting the bridle on in one piece, always make sure you push the ears forward as you bring the headpiece over them. If the ears are allowed to remain back the headpiece is likely to come to rest on top of the ears, squeezing them, and this can make the horse head-shy.

If possible horses should not be turned out to grass day and night with their headcollars on. Colts in particular are liable to get hold of each others' headcollars in play and chew or pull them off. There is also the danger that an animal could get its headcollar caught on a fence or tree. So unless you are very certain you would never be able to catch the young horse again if you removed its headcollar, all headcollars should be taken off when the animals are released. Many studs remove headcollars as a routine every night and replace them just before turning out in the morning. This accustoms young horses to being handled round the head and so makes bridling easier.

It is debatable whether it is necessary to teach yearlings to tie up. However, if you do decide to tie yours up, care must be taken to ensure that a breakable headcollar is used and that the rope is attached to a piece of baler-twine and not straight on to the metal ring. This will ensure that something breaks before the horse's neck does, should it get frightened, run back and slip over. For the first few weeks a young horse should never be left on its own when tied up. It usually helps if a small feed is provided or the animal is scratched or brushed over if it enjoys this. Ensure there is plenty of bedding on the floor.

Yearlings may be introduced to the idea of wearing a roller each day. First of all, get the young horse used to the feel of something round its middle, by passing a web leading rein round the girth area. In the meantime select a sound roller fitted with a breast girth. Most young horses give a lively rodeo display the first time a roller is put on. Without a breast girth the roller could work back as the youngster tries to buck it off. Some people also fit a crupper to stabilise the roller. If the horse has a bad shoulder and flat withers a crupper may be essential, otherwise it is considered unnecessary and could encourage bucking.

To put the roller on for the first time, use a fully enclosed straw yard, lungeing ring or large well-bedded loose-box. Two people are preferable. Stand the horse close to the door and ensure that the person holding the horse is standing on the near-side of its head, ready to turn its quarters away from the second person, if necessary. Hold the horse quite still. Few horses start bucking when the roller is put on for the first time until they move a step or two. Place the roller across the horse's back; fasten the breast girth first and then the roller itself, until the latter is just tight enough to be secure. Slip the rein from the headcollar, but hold the horse still with the headcollar itself until the first person is out of the yard or lungeing ring. Then the second person can let the horse loose and 'beat a hasty retreat'. If the horse has been lunged previously, it may be allowed to run round you now on the lunge.

71

Some horses do not react at all to the pressure of the roller, whereas others buck and kick violently, or just stand still and sulk. Preferably leave the roller on all night. Otherwise before removing it, catch the horse, put the rein through the headcollar and lead it round. Keep a tight hold of the headcollar as walking may precipitate a rodeo display. If the horse is relaxed and walking quietly, ask your helper to hold its head, again standing to the near-side. Un-buckle the roller and then the breast girth. Remove the roller carefully, making sure that you do not frighten the horse.

The roller should be put on the young horse every day for about an hour and the animal either led round inside its loose-box, taken for a short walk or lunged, before the roller is removed.

Rollers accustom young horses to pressure round the girth area and therefore act as a preliminary introduction to wearing a rug or saddle. They are further used as an aid to mouthing and an additional means of control when lungeing and long-reining.

Once the young horse is quite used to wearing both a bridle and roller each day, side-reins may be introduced. All side-reins are adjustable but it helps if the holes are numbered, as they must be kept the same length both sides.

Fit the side-reins either by passing the roller through the loops, if it has no D's, or by buckling the side-reins to the top D's on the roller. The latter method is preferable as it means the side-reins can be fitted after the roller is in place. Cross the reins over the base of the neck, just in front of the withers. Adjust the length, so that they fit loosely. Check that they are exactly the same length before buckling or clipping them to the bit rings. The slight pressure exerted when the horse stretches or lowers its head encourages it to mouth the bit. Do not shorten the reins at this stage or leave the bit and side-reins on for more than an hour, otherwise the horse's mouth could become sore.

When young horses are shown regularly or prepared for sale, rugs or sheets are sometimes used to preserve their summer coats. A well-padded roller made from either web or leather is preferable to a surcingle. It is important to ensure that there is sufficient padding in the roller to prevent pressure on the spine. The rug should be fitted with keepers either side to hold the roller in place. If keepers are used, the roller will not slip and cause a sore back.

72

A surcingle is normally sewn on to the rug some 10 inches (25cm) behind the roller. This helps to hold the rug in place, particularly when the horse tries to buck it off. Most rugs are fitted with eyelets to take a fillet string.

The same precautions must be taken when putting a rug on for the first time as were taken for the roller alone. Once a horse has become accustomed to wearing a roller he normally does not react when the rug is put on, but some repeat their rodeo display so care must be taken.

As before, choose a straw or sand yard, lungeing ring, or well-bedded large loose-box. Ask your assistant to hold the horse near the door standing to the near-side of the horse.

Fold the rug so that the neck part is exposed, until it is a little wider than the roller. Place the folded rug across the horse's back as you would the roller. Fasten the breast strap. Gradually unroll the rug over the back and the quarters, stroking the back and talking to the horse. Fasten the roller and then the loin surcingle; the latter should be left some three holes slacker than the roller. To remove the rug, reverse the order: un-buckle the surcingle, then the roller and finally the breast strap. This prevents the rug sliding back should the horse buck.

Never try to put a sheet or rug on a young horse outside on a windy day or approach it with an open rug and throw it across its back as you would an old hunter. New rugs are normally stiff, so should be washed before use on young horses.

Ideally, young horses should not be lunged until their leg epiphyses have closed (18 – 24 months old). In the meantime they can be educated to walk out smartly when led. In this respect mechanical horse walkers cannot replace human beings.

Unshod horses should not be led for long periods on a hard surface otherwise they may become footsore. Yearlings tend to jump about and therefore could knock their legs if boots are not worn – at least on the front legs. Felt polo boots afford the greatest protection, are easy to put on and seldom slip down the leg.

To school a horse to walk out when asked, carry a long stick (about the length of a dressage whip) in your left hand. If the horse hangs back or fails to walk on, click or use a word of command. If this is ignored, repeat the word or click and at the same time give the horse a sharp reminder on its quarters, without altering your

(a)

(b)

The judge or buyers will look for a long, free stride at the walk. The hind feet should track up to the imprint left by the fore feet (a). This can only be achieved with a very light contact on the bit: the weight of the rein is normally sufficient. Impulsion comes from the hindquarters not the front end. If the horse lowers its head and 'goes to sleep', the leader should activate it again by clicking or giving the horse a sharp reminder on its hindquarters. The impulsion created in the hindquarters will automatically raise the head and lengthen the stride in front as well as behind.

(b) Some people incorrectly raise the head by shaking the rein just below the horse's jaw. This causes the horse to hollow its back and shorten its stride.

74

position by its shoulder; hence the length of the stick. Horses soon learn to associate the one with the other and quickly come to obey your voice alone.

For maximum control of a fresh horse use your right elbow against the front of the horse's shoulder. Pass the rein tightly across your body to your left hand which is held against your left hip or behind your back. *Never wrap the rein round your hand.*

Horses should always be led in a clockwise direction and never anti-clockwise, for the following two reasons:

(1) The pressure of your elbow against the neck and shoulder helps to steady the horse and push it away from you. Full control can therefore be maintained during all turns to the right but is partly lost when turning left.

(2) Horses tend to jump away from anything which frightens them. When walking in a circle more frightening things are likely to occur on the outside than the inside of the circle. The horse will, therefore, jump away from its leader.

It is safer to lead young horses with bits in their mouths. To obtain a light even pressure a three-way coupling should be used. The centre strap links the noseband and the throatlash with the bit strap. The lead rein passes through the large ring in the centre. Pressure is therefore exerted simultaneously on the mouth, nose and poll. The lower a noseband is adjusted the more control it affords. Nosebands must however, remain on the nasal bones otherwise a direct pull would restrict the horse's breathing. The poll is sensitive to pressure so a pull on the throatlash enhances control.

When the centre strap is attached to the throatlash the coupling cannot catch the bottom lip. This method of attachment will also improve the appearance of a heavy jaw bone.

When schooling or exercising young horses at home, it is safer to thread the rein through the centre ring of the coupling rather than buckle it onto the bit. Initially walking should take place in a quiet paddock, away from other horses, *with the gate shut.*

A very light contact on the lead-rein or a loose rein will encourage most horses to settle and walk quietly.

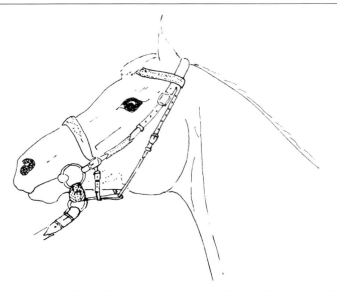

FIG 19a Safely fitted three-way coupling (Paddy Burns' method). Exerts pressure simultaneously on the mouth, noseband and poll.

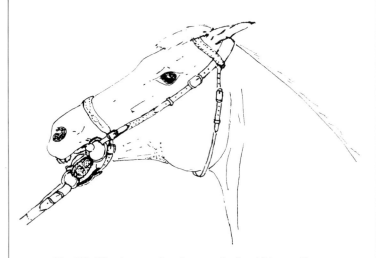

FIG 19b The danger of an incorrectly fitted bit coupling.

(a)

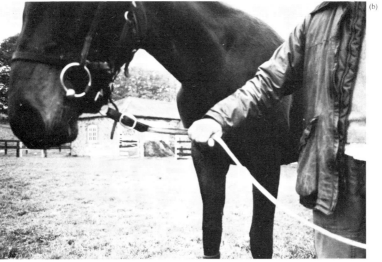

(b)

(a) The correct and (b) incorrect method of holding the rein when leading a horse. Just as when riding a horse, the hand must be light and responsive to the movements of the horse's head and neck. This movement is particularly pronounced at the walk. The hand must therefore be able to give and take instantaneously, in most cases only using the flexion of the wrist. Or, when the horse is relaxed, allowing the rein to slide backwards and forwards through the palm of your right hand. This is virtually impossible when the rein is held as shown in photograph (b).

77

CHAPTER TEN

Notes on buying thoroughbred foals and selling yearlings

A GREAT DEAL OF money can be made, or lost, by buying foals in November or December to sell ten months later as yearlings. It is obviously much easier to make a profit in a rising market, particularly when times are good, but with careful planning and a certain amount of luck, money can be made, even in a bad year.

Foals must be selected with a particular sale in mind. If you have never sold yearlings before make an appointment to see the auctioneers before the foal sales or speak to them on the telephone. Discuss the possibility of places in the major yearling sales and the standard of individual required by the sales company concerned. Most cater for at least 3 categories of yearling:

> 1. The select/invitational yearlings, which are elite individuals;
> 2. The premier yearlings, with above average conformation and pedigree;
> 3. Open sales yearlings, with average conformation and/or pedigree;
> 4. Yearlings with major conformation faults or weak pedigrees are normally sent to mixed sales.

Before investing any money in foals, it would be wise to attend at least one major yearling sale — note the fashionable bloodlines and standard of presentation. The art of foal buying is being able to predict what is likely to be fashionable and therefore in demand the following year. Some people have a real flair for this, as well as a good eye for a horse, but there are several factors which if taken into consideration can improve your chances of 'hitting the jackpot'. Many people employ the services of a successful bloodstock agent, whereas others prefer to select their own foals and enjoy the preliminary homework this entails. In the latter case, you should obtain copies of all the yearling sales returns from the autioneers or buy a copy of a Yearling Sales Index for the year — published soon after the last major yearling sale. The Sales Index not only gives you the average price of the yearlings by each stallion but also the median — which is a better guide for foal buyers.

Buy a copy of *The Statistical Record Return of Mares*, which covers the year relating to the yearling sales, and the *Timeform Black Book*, final issue for the year.

When you receive the foal sales catalogues, go through them; assess the catalogues and mark each animal in which you are interested. Go back to the beginning and note:

(1) The yearling out of the same dam, it's sire, how much it made if it was sold, and most important of all, who bought it — the trainer will have some significance in gauging its chances of winning the following year. If the yearling was bought for export, find out the country and assess it's significance in the 'pecking order' of international racing. If the yearling was not sold, you can note the breeder and this may give you some clue to the likely trainer.

If the second dam is young enough to have a yearling, this too should be traced.

(2) Next, look up the current 2-year-old's form in the *Black Book*. If the animal is not a winner, you will have to make up your own mind regarding its chances of winning at 3 years. Obviously the more winners which appear in the pedigree *after* you have bought your foal the better your chance of making a profit, particularly if they are European Pattern or foreign Graded Race winners.

(3) Check the sires and mentally give them a 'fashion rating', eliminating all those from your list which you know or believe will be unfashionable in a year's time. Turn to the index of foals under their sires and enter the following information: The stud fee for each horse; the median price of the yearlings sold that year and the number of live foals the previous year — this will give you

an idea of the number of 2 year old runners. Note the first and second season sires.

If you do not wish to gamble on the possible demand for a particular sire's progeny, it is safer to buy foals by an established sire or a first-season sire — there is usually a demand for good looking progeny by the latter.

If on the other hand you like to have a gamble buy foals by sires which are going to have their first runners the next year. If the sire is a failure you will be left with 'a dead duck'; but if he is a success then you will probably make a good profit. You can reduce the odds slightly by studying the list of mares the stallion in question received in his first season and assessing the chances of the live foals becoming 2-year-old winners. Again, check which trainers have the yearlings. A large number of foals reduces their rarity value but gives the horse a better chance of producing winners.

(4) Finally go through the foals and see which, if any, are closely related to an individual you think might make a top-class 3-year-old, or from your researches among the yearlings, a top-class 2-year-old the following year.

You are now armed with a list of possible candidates. To save time when examining these foals, 'dog ear' the catalogue or mark the lot numbers.

Examine each foal carefully, for conformation and soundness. This must be done systematically, otherwise it is very easy to miss some important point — foals are always sold as they stand, without any warranty except for wind sucking or as stated in the conditions of sale. Devise your own inspection chart and code, an example is given below:

General impression:
Height: Bone:
Head: Mouth:
Genital organs: Pelvis:
Legs:
Feet: Action:
Temperament:
Heart: Eyes:

First impressions are very important so it is useful to use a rating system — say *, ** or *** — according to how much you like the foal. Yearling buyers will also be influenced by their first impression; as most will not have time to see if the animal grows on them, instant appeal is essential.

Foals are usually quieter to handle before they have been taken out of their loose-boxes. This is the time to check the mouth, genital organs, bone and height, also to look for any lumps, bumps or malformations.

Many foals' mouths are very slightly over-shot; most are fully in contact by the time they are yearlings, but true parrot-mouths seldom come right.

When examining colts check that both testicles are visible or can be felt. If it is impossible to either see or feel both, it would be wise to have the animal examined by a veterinary surgeon before purchase. There is less demand for yearling rigs than for colts.

To gauge potential size at maturity, the withers height must be related to the date of birth, condition, general conformation and rump height.

Ask the person in charge if you might see the animal outside. First stand the foal four-square on level ground, with the sun behind you. Note its general outlook. If you like what you see, examine the legs, head, neck, shoulders, back and hind-quarters. Stand directly behind the animal and check its pelvis and hind-legs. Stand in front of the foal to check the front legs and feet, and note any deviations, or defects.

Since most wobblers are incapable of backing, reverse the foal actively for at least three strides, then spin it in a tight circle in both directions. Look for signs of inco-ordination or lameness. Walk and if possible trot the foal to check that it is sound, has a long stride and moves straight.

Only gamble on straightening a turned foot if you have the services of a good blacksmith, and then only if the deviation is not due to a twisted joint or bent leg. Note if any corrective trimming has already taken place and assess the effect obtained. If the front feet are not quite a pair, it could be that the foal has been scraping the floor, but be careful as few people will want a yearling with boxy or odd feet.

If possible have the foal walked round you in a circle. 'The time you buy is the time you sell', therefore do not be in too great a hurry to rush on to the next animal.

Ask a veterinary surgeon to examine the hearts, eyes and testicles (where applicable) of all the foals on your 'short-list'.

It pays to arrange insurance before buying foals, then cover will be in effect from the fall of the hammer. Wind insurance can usually be included.

If possible follow the foals you buy out of the sale ring and speak to the owners or stud grooms to ascertain any useful information concerning the individuals, especially their diet. Ask the previous owners if they would be kind enough to feed them for you and leave the foals with ample hay and water — most do this automatically. It is up to the buyer or his shipping agent, to provide headcollars for animals purchased at bloodstock sales. If the previous owner tells you a foal may be difficult to catch, it would be wise to ask him to put your headcollar on the foal before he leaves.

Collect the foal markings and vaccination certificates from the auctioneers' office and compare the individuals with the markings shown in the diagrams. Should there be any significant discrepancy, notify the auctioneers immediately. However, some firms now check these themselves before the animals are sold.

Observe the foals, check especially that none shows evidence of crib-biting, windsucking or weaving. Stable vices for which animals may be returned vary from one sales company to the next so check the conditions in the catalogue. Purchasers are usually allowed 7 days from the last day of the sale to return any lot, under this clause.

Worm the foals, before moving them from the sale yard or as soon as they arrive home but before turning them out. Unvaccinated foals should receive their primary injection against tetanus and 'flu, as soon as possible.

Some foals which have been prepared for the sales may have been stabled for the previous 4 weeks, so care must be taken when they are first turned out. Choose a well-fenced paddock and turn two foals out together, waiting until they have settled before adding another one. If all the foals are turned out at the same time one might well gallop through or over a fence.

Do not remove the headcollars when you turn the foals out,

Thoroughbred sales yearlings returning home after at least an hour's exercise across open farmland.

otherwise you may have difficulty catching them again. They should soon settle down in their new surroundings and become used to the people who are looking after them each day.

Yearlings may be left out day and night once the weather is warmer and the grass is growing – normally between the end of March and mid-April. They must, however, come in at least 6 weeks before their sales.

Pedigree details which appear in the catalogue can influence the price an animal makes. Some sales companies make their own arrangements regarding pedigree details, even so it pays to have your pedigrees compiled or checked by a professional who has access to the international racing results.

In order to make a name for your stud and be a success you should only submit your best animals for the major sales. Inferior individuals which would spoil the overall standard of the draft should be sold elsewhere. If, one year, you only have poor individuals to offer, safeguard your stud's good name and send them to a minor sale. Contrary to popular belief, by doing this you will not lose your place in the major sales.

Animals being prepared for show or sale should never be bedded down with barley straw, as this tends to cause rubbing. Wheat straw is the best bedding material, although peat moss may be used; however nothing shows a horse off so well to potential buyers as a deep straw bed.

Once the yearlings have been brought in they should be walked for at least an hour a day. Boots must be worn on the forelegs as a protection against last-minute knocks. For the first quarter of an hour or so, the young horses should be walked round a paddock, with the gate closed. Once they have settled and are leading well, to alleviate boredom, they can be taken round the stud.

Manes must be pulled. A pulled tail helps to accentuate round quarters but the regular use of a damp tail bandage for a few hours improves the appearance of an un-pulled tail. The bottom of the tail should be pulled so that it lies just below the hock joint. Any long hairs in the ears should be removed.

Horses must be taught to stand correctly and remain stationary until asked to walk on. They should also be taught to trot when asked. Running a horse up in-hand must be practised at home and if necessary a stick can be carried to ensure that the horse trots when required.

At most sales it is customary, and also a great help to the buyers, to have door cards printed giving details of each lot. These usually measure about 12 inches (30cm) by 20 inches (50cm). They should be kept as simple as possible, and include recent pedigree information.

Make arrangements for your animals to arrive at the sales as early as possible and not less than 3 days before they are sold. It normally takes young horses at least a day to settle in new surroundings. Buyers often start inspecting lots at least 3 days before the commencement of the sale, therefore it pays to arrive in good time.

Give the animals hay, water and a feed when they arrive and leave them to settle before removing any sweat marks. Examine the area in the immediate vicinity of your loose-boxes. Bearing in mind that the sun should not be in the buyers' eyes, select a place

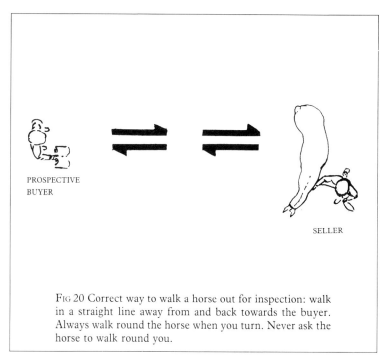

PROSPECTIVE
BUYER

SELLER

FIG 20 Correct way to walk a horse out for inspection: walk
in a straight line away from and back towards the buyer.
Always walk round the horse when you turn. Never ask the
horse to walk round you.

which will show your animals off to best advantage and find the
most level ground to walk your horses.

Organise your staff so that there is someone in attendance from
seven in the morning until about six o'clock in the evening.
Where more than one person is employed at the sales, meal times
should be staggered. If the horses are left unattended for any
reason, a note should be placed on the loose-box doors giving the
time someone will return.

As far as possible do not alter the horses' diet when they are at
the sales. If their coats are shining as a result of good feeding, they
will need very little last-minute grooming. A damp body brush
will remove any surface dust and grease from the coat and a quick
wipe over with a coarse stable rubber will produce a good shine.
White markings can be cleaned with chalk and hooves should be
oiled. Ensure that your staff also look smart. Keep the area in
front of your loose-boxes clean, as this gives an impression of
efficiency. Gravel paths must be raked to remove straw and hoof
prints; concrete should be swept clean.

Young horses should be schooled to stand correctly, and show themselves to best advantage. For instance, a horse will appear to have a greater length of rein if it is encouraged to stretch its neck. (N.B. Boots should always be worn at exercise.)

Make sure all relevant documents, such as foal identification and veterinary certificates for wind, have been lodged with the auctioneers before the sale starts. Also remember to fix your reserves. As a general rule high reserves tend to deter buyers.

Remember, whether your animals have sold well or not, it is good manners to find the auctioneer afterwards and thank him for doing his best to sell your horses.

CHAPTER ELEVEN

Castration

CASTRATION IS THE removal of the male sex organs, the testicles, in order to render the animal more docile and easy to handle. It also removes both the primary and secondary male characteristics, to a greater or lesser extent, depending on the age of the animal when the operation is carried out. When colts are castrated as yearlings they do not develop a crest, the typical voice of the stallion or his naturally aggressive nature. Castration renders male horses safe to ride and turn out with mares; in some cases it also makes the animal a better jumper.

The castrated male horse is known as a gelding. The operation must be performed by your veterinary surgeon, and cannot be done until both testicles have decended into the scrotum. In the majority of cases the testicles are in the scrotum at birth, but sometimes they do not appear until the animal is about 18 months to 2 years old. Occasionally animals are found with only one testicle descended, and more rarely still with neither descended. These animals are known as rigs, or more correctly cryptorchids; those with one testicle down being referred to as monorchids.

Castration is best carried out in the spring once the frosty nights have gone and before the flies come out, or in the autumn when the flies have gone and before the frosts have started. The horse should be starved the night before the operation, particularly if a general anaesthetic is to be used. If the operation is to be performed at home, select a clean well-fenced paddock, free from stones and obstacles. The site chosen must be well away from a fence, to reduce the risk of injury when the horse goes down and when it comes round.

Castration may be performed under either: (a) general anaesthetic, with the animal on the ground; or (b) local anaesthetic, with the animal standing. Many owners prefer the operation to be done under a local anaesthetic, but animals must be well handled and respond to discipline if there is not to be a risk both to your colt and the veterinary surgeon. A general anaesthetic is essential for 'rigs' and also where a hernia into the scrotal sac is suspected. If castration was carried out under these circumstances in the standing position, the intestines would drop through the cut and the animal might well have to be destroyed.

When the operation has been performed under a general anaesthetic, somebody should stay with the animal until he has come round. A lungeing rein should be attached to the headcollar so that the horse can be controlled when he comes to, but care should be taken that the attendant does not get too close to the horse in the early stages otherwise the animal might fall on top of him in his efforts to get up. Once the horse is standing he can be walked around for several minutes and then loosed in the middle of the paddock.

Exercise is of great importance following castration as it helps to reduce swelling in the hind legs and scrotum. Horses which for any reason have to be housed after castration, *must be lunged every day* and must be kept on very clean bedding. Should the scrotum start to swell unduly your veterinary surgeon must be called in immediately as some infection may be present. It is a good idea to take the animal's temperature every day for about 10 days so that any slight rise can be noted before signs of infection or general septicaemia become apparent.

The castration of 'rigs' (cryptorchids) may involve a major abdominal operation, as the undescended testicle sometimes lies inside the body cavity.

Uncastrated 'rigs' are usually most undesirable animals; some are capable of getting mares in-foal and exhibit many male characteristics, including screaming and striking with their front legs.

Where valuable pedigree stock are concerned it is often better to leave them uncastrated until they have proved their worth (or otherwise) on the racecourse or in the show-ring. Nothing is more infuriating than to own a champion gelding, which would have

been worth many thousands of pounds more as a stallion. Therefore, as a rule, all pedigree stock of sufficient merit should be left
uncastrated until the end of their yearling year or, in the case of
'flat' racehorses, until at least the end of their 2-year-old season.
It is usual to castrate all other horses as as foals or yearlings.

CHAPTER TWELVE

Management of the store horse

A STORE HORSE is any horse which, for economic reasons, does not need to be broken before it is completely mature. It can therefore be kept (stored) until it is at least 3 years old before it is broken and ridden.

The degree of maturity attained by any horse at a given age is mainly due to two factors: heredity and environment.

Most horses do not become mature enough to ride until they are at least 3 years old and therefore should not be broken until this age. Ridden classes at shows are confined to horses of 4 years and over for this reason.

As mentioned in Chapter 3, the epiphyses or growth plates at the lower extremities of the long bones (radius and tibia) in the horse's legs do not close finally until the animal is at least 18 months old. The epiphysis at the end of the cannon bone — immediately above the fetlock joint — is usually closed by the time the foal is about 9 – 12 months old, whereas the epiphysis at the elbow joint (olecranon) does not close until the animal is about 24–30 months old. When yearling buyers describe an apparently immature individual as having 'open knees', they are referring to the extent to which the epiphysis at the bottom of the radius is closing. Since this is the last noticeable growing point in the limbs to close, it acts as a guide to the general maturity of young horse. It is impossible to tell with certainty exactly when the epiphyses have closed by visual examination alone. Therefore many people now ask their veterinary surgeons to x-ray the growth plates at the end of the radius of valuable youngstock before they put them into work. It is also common practice in America, when thoroughbred yearlings are sold at public auction, to have x-rays of the growth plates on display.

If an animal is worked before the epiphyses have closed, inflammation may be produced which results in a soft swelling just above the knee joint (in yearlings), mainly on the inside of the leg (see Fig. 8). If the animal remains in work, the epiphysis gets wider, the inflammation spreads, fibrous tissue forms and bony enlargements appear. In all probability the animal will not go lame initially, but some pain will be shown if the swellings are pressed. In the long term, arthritis may develop.

Ideally, horses should be allowed to mature slowly and not be rushed at any period of their development. The very worst thing one can do to a foal, in fact, is to prepare it for a sale. A store foal or yearling which is not going to be broken until it is about 4 years old should be allowed to mature naturally at an even rate of growth. This will eliminate the harmful side effects which can be created by over-fattening a young horse before its skeletal development is complete. For ease of management store colts are usually gelded as yearlings, but some people prefer to geld all their colt foals.

Store horses are usually sold as unbroken 3 to 4 year-olds, when they have normally attained their greatest value as young horses. As this entails keeping them for some 3 – 4 years, the overall costs of production must be kept within reasonable limits. Sufficient grazing must be available throughout the year, otherwise the production of store horses is better not attempted. High labour and feeding costs would make for a very uneconomic enterprise.

Basically there are three methods of keeping young store horses:

Out day and night throughout the year
Most horses stand dry cold weather but few do well when it is both cold and wet. Therefore, where possible, field shelters should be provided. These should be sited with their backs to the prevailing wind, on a very well-drained, dry base. They can be equipped with hay racks and feed troughs so that the horses can be fed inside the shelter during the winter months, but all field shelters should have open fronts so that any horse which is being bullied by its companions has a readily available means of escape, without which serious accidents can happen, especially at feeding time.

When horses are to remain out during the winter, the driest and most sheltered field on the farm should be chosen. Horses tend to poach land badly when the weather is wet, so cracked heels must be looked for and, if they occur, treated immediately with a preparation supplied by your veterinary surgeon, otherwise severe inflammation and lameness (mud fever) may develop. Young horses must be kept in reasonable condition throughout the year so that they can grow and mature normally. A careful watch must therefore be kept on the amount and quality of grass available. The easiest way to feed horses at grass is to use a Land-Rover to cart bales of hay or bags of nuts out to the fields. Land-Rovers are safer than tractors and trailers, as there is always the possibility that one of the horses could get pushed over the trailer bar by its companions. As a rough guide allow one bale of hay between two to four animals and ½ cwt (25 kilos) nuts between eight animals, according to the amount and value of grass available.

Drop the hay and nuts off in piles across the field, allowing at least three more piles of each than animals in the paddock to prevent fighting. Choose the cleanest and most sheltered areas, giving sufficient room between the various piles and the nearest fence or hedge so that bullied animals do not find themselves trapped. Alternatively the food can be placed in the field shelter, or in metal food troughs fixed on to the fence. Salt licks or lumps of rock salt should be made available at all times throughout the year. As far as possible, animals of a similar size should be placed together. It would be asking for trouble to run weaned foals with strong 3-year-olds, particularly when they are to be fed together. You will be able to judge when to stop feeding the horses in the spring as they will no longer clean up the hay.

During frosty weather the water troughs must be inspected at least twice a day and the ice broken when necessary so that the horses never go short of water. Make sure that any automatic filling device still works — external pipes are better lagged before the hard weather comes. Chalk can be placed around the water troughs and gateways to help reduce poaching.

Yarding the horses during the winter months
Deep-litter bedding should be used and the covered yard mucked out in the spring after the horses have been turned out to grass.

Obviously this must not be a low-roofed building as it would have to be mucked out several times during the winter.

Horses, unlike ruminants, do not thrive on a high-fibre diet, so yarded horses fed nothing but hay, unless it is very good quality, will lose weight. Feed troughs should be sited down side walls of the yard allowing at least 10 feet (3m) per horse. Salt licks should be provided, and a suitable water trough, which must be cleaned out regularly. Adequate ventilation is essential, as stuffy conditions lead to respiratory troubles; a half-open yard is ideal if well sheltered.

When horses are yarded together it is important not to mix the sizes too drastically, particularly weaned foals with older horses otherwise accidents might happen. Allow 150 square feet (45.5×45.5m) of floor area per animal.

Yarding has the advantage that the horses are not out on the land when it is very wet and therefore will not be cutting the fields up, or developing cracked heels. An earlier bite will be obtained in the spring if the paddocks remain empty all winter. Horses' feet must be attended to regularly when the animals are running out at grass all the year round or yarded on deep litter. There is no natural wear of the hoof wall on soft ground, so the hoof may start to grow out of shape if neglected, and this can be difficult to correct later.

Kept in loose-boxes during the winter, turned out each day
If the loose-boxes are mucked out each day the labour requirements would be too high for store horses; that is unless the owner looks on the enterprise as a hobby and does all the work alone. Otherwise deep litter must be used.

By bringing the horses in every day they can be handled regularly and therefore should not become wild. If labour is short, lead the horses out individually in the morning. A shoot formed from a series of hurdles may be necessary so that one person can turn out a large number of horses on his or her own each day and, bring them in each evening without help. The other advantage of this system is that individual horses get a known amount of food, and greedy horses cannot get fat at the expense of their more fastidious companions.

Even if animals are kept in fields all their lives, some loose-box accommodation must be available. Sick or injured animals may need to be brough inside at any time. Most young horses are easier to cope with if they are housed to have their feet trimmed. This does also mean that the young horses are handled from time to time.

Good-looking youngstock can be shown throughout the summer months. If they are taken to a few shows each year you will find that they are virtually broken by the time they are 3 years old. As a rough guide, for hunter classes at county show level, colt foals should measure 14.2 h.h. by the turn of the year and fillies some 2 inches (5cm) less. By the time they are 2 years old they should be about 16.0 h.h.

Some of the bloodstock sales companies organise special sales for stock with potential as National Hunt horses (horses likely to win races over hurdles and fences). They will usually accept half-bred horses as well as thoroughbreds, so long as they have some potential as racehorses, even if it is only as point-to-pointers. The most important sales are held about the beginning of June; these include:

Doncaster Bloodstock Sales — Spring Sale, mid-May.
J. P. Botterill's — Ascot sale, at the beginning of June.
Doncaster Bloodstock Sales — "York Race" Sales, mid-August.
Ballsbridge Tattersalls Sales — Derby Sale, at the end of June.
Goffs — Punchestown Festival Sale, at the end of April.
  (These sales are usually preceded by in-hand show classes for
  unraced 3 and 4-year-olds likely to make high-class National
  Hunt horses.)
Ballsbridge Sales — Dublin Horse Show Sales, for owners of exhibited horses, not necessarily with any potential as racehorses but rather as good riding horses, hunters, show jumpers, etc.

Many of the breed societies also hold their own sales each year for registered stock.

CHAPTER THIRTEEN

The art of loading and travelling horses by road

Most horses and ponies travel by road some time during their lives, and those bred specifically for showing, hunting or racing will probably spend a large portion of their time on the road. They should therefore become accustomed to loading and travelling from an early age.

It is essential to have some facilities for loading and unloading horses on a stud. Even if you only own a trailer yourself, you should make provision for horse-boxes, as these are sure to visit your stud to collect or deliver a horse one day. All trailers are fitted with low-loading ramps, so measure the height of the trailer's ramp before building a loading ramp or select a quiet spot where you can run the trailer tight up against one wall of a building, but make sure that the trailer really is tight up against the wall, otherwise a horse might get a leg down between the ramp and the wall and injure itself. In the case of horse-boxes, it is almost essential to build a loading ramp.

The ramp should be sited in such a position on the stud that large horse-boxes have plenty of room to turn round, and the ground in front of the ramp must be solid enough to take the weight of heavy vehicles even in wet weather. Most horse-boxes have their loading ramps on the near side of the vehicle, so they must have room to pull up straight alongside the ramp on this side.

It is much easier to load horses in a quiet place away from other animals, so loading ramps should be built out of sight of the paddocks. For this reason it is also better to close-board the shute which leads to the ramp itself. This shute should be made in such a way that the ground level gradually rises to meet the height of

96

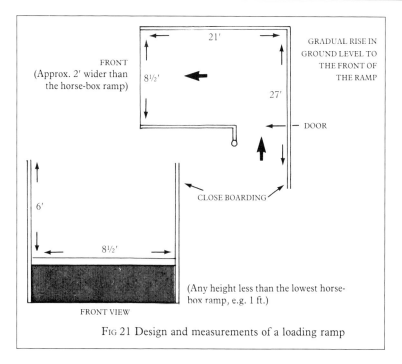

FIG 21 Design and measurements of a loading ramp

the ramp. The surface should be well drained and preferably grassed over, or have some other form of non-slip surface. This is particularly important when unloading, as some horses have the habit of jumping down from the top of ramps. Shutes should also be made long enough so that horses can be walked into them easily when a horse-box is in position for loading, and sited so that horses do not have to pass the vehicle.

Before travelling mares with foals at foot, the following points should be borne in mind:

Where the foal has access to the front of the trailer or is to be travelled in a groom's compartment, the groom's door must be securely locked from the outside to prevent any chance of the foal opening the door from the inside by leaning on the handle.

Windows which are low enough to be reached by the foal must be fitted with a wire-mesh guard to prevent any chance of the foal injuring itself.

Where mares are to be travelled with foals at foot, the centre partition should be removed from two-horse trailers to convert

97

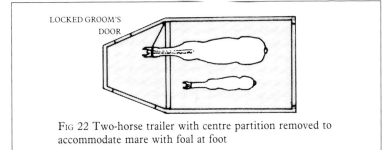

Fig 22 Two-horse trailer with centre partition removed to accommodate mare with foal at foot

them into a single loose-box; the same applies to horse-boxes (see Fig.22). In the case of trailers it is essential that a metal breast bar is fitted, so that the mare is not thrown to the front of the trailer whenever the brakes are applied. The mare must be tied up but the foal should be travelled loose, preferably without a headcollar, so that it cannot get caught up on anything during the journey. The breast bar can be padded with foam rubber for extra protection when the foal walks underneath. As foals mostly travel lying down, the floor should be well bedded down with straw.

If hay-nets are uses in horse-boxes or trailers, they must be tied up as tightly and as high as possible, preferably using two strings. They must be checked periodically during the journey as if they drop down a horse could easily get a leg through the net.

Mares should not be travelled in stalls or single-horse trailers with foals at foot as there is insufficient room, unless the foal is placed in the front of the trailer, with a hinged solid partition between it and the mare, or in the groom's compartment of a horse-box (see Fig.23). If a foal is placed in the groom's

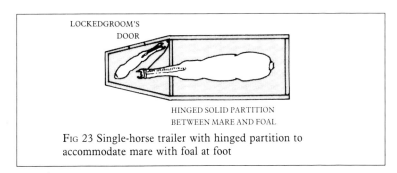

Fig 23 Single-horse trailer with hinged partition to accommodate mare with foal at foot

compartment, no other horse should be travelled in such a position that it can bite the foal. In the case of young foals, under a month old, a stop must be made at least once every 2 hours, to allow them to suck the mare. Older foals can go a little longer without milk.

When travelling mares with foals at foot, both trailer ramp top doors should be kept closed in cold weather to help eliminate any draughts, and in the case of older foals to prevent any chance of their jumping out during the journey. However, in hot weather some ventilation must be provided. To achieve this the left-hand top door should be fastened back or removed and replaced with fine-mesh wire-netting (see Fig.24). This should be tied on to the door hinges and fastenings and will provide sufficient air, at the same time preventing any chance of the foal jumping out. The off-side top door should be kept closed so that the mare is not encouraged to turn round and also to cut out the sight of over-taking traffic.

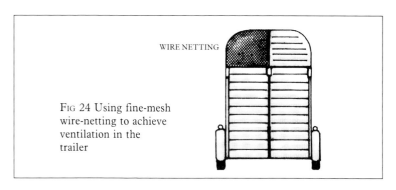

WIRE NETTING

FIG 24 Using fine-mesh wire-netting to achieve ventilation in the trailer

Loading horses into trailers and horse-boxes can be a very difficult task unless a little horse-sense and tact is applied. Then what seemed previously to be an impossible task suddenly becomes easy.

Most horses are willing to co-operate if they feel they are in a confined space with little room or opportunity to play up. To this end a loading ramp as already described is an almost essential piece of equipment to facilitate the loading of animals into horse-boxes. As far as trailers are concerned, the great thing to remember is that unless the animal is known to be easy to load, one should not try to load it in the middle of an open space, but should site the trailer close to a wall or in a confined gateway. Leaving the front ramp top door open lets more light into the trailer and sometimes helps a nervous horse.

Horses do not like to step on to a surface which is not absolutely solid. Therefore ramps should be checked to make sure that they are level and that there is no movement. If the ramp is not on level ground, pieces of flat stone or wood should be placed under it until there is no possible movement when someone walks on the ramp.

Young or inexperienced horses can be encouraged to walk on to a ramp more easily if the trailer or horse-box, its ramp and the immediate area in front of the ramp are covered with straw. This makes it look less frightening. A vehicle ramp should have the minimum slope — hence the use of a loading ramp. As far as possible, inexperienced or nervous horses should be given the maximum width of stall to walk into. To achieve this, the partition should be moved to one side, and replaced once the horse is loaded (see Fig.25). Then the breaching strap should be fastened before the centre partition is secured, or the back ramp put up, otherwise the horse might become frightened and attempt to run out backwards as the partition is moved.

When loading horses into vehicles and trailers, the handler should walk by the horse's head and on no account should he turn to look at the horse, as nothing is calculated to stop a horse quicker than to turn round and look him in the face. The handler should not duck under the bar until the breaching strap has been fastened by an assistant or the back ramp has been put up, otherwise if the horse decides to reverse out of the trailer or horse-box suddenly, the handler will be compelled to let the horse go. For the same reason, the horse should not be tied up until his exit is securely barred, otherwise he would almost certainly break his headcollar.

To counteract the natural camber of the road, when only one horse is being travelled in a two-horse trailer or horse-box it should be loaded into the off-side stall. When more than one horse is to be travelled at the same time, the heavier one should be put on the off side. In the case of mares with foals at foot, the foal is left loose but the mare should be tied to the off-side ring in the horse-box or trailer. When tying horses, the rope should be

100

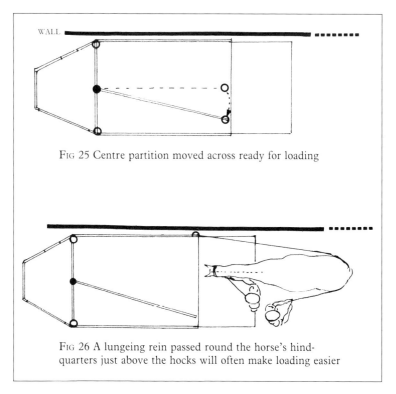

Fig 25 Centre partition moved across ready for loading

Fig 26 A lungeing rein passed round the horse's hind-quarters just above the hocks will often make loading easier

secured with a slip knot which can be untied quickly. When two or more horses are being travelled, head boards should be fitted, or the horses secured so that they cannot touch noses, otherwise they might start fighting during the journey. To prevent the head-collar from being broken in the event of a horse pulling back suddenly, some people fasten a loop of baler twine to the ring in the vehicle and tie the rope to the twine.

Horses which are reluctant to load are often encouraged to do so if a lungeing rein is fastened to the far side of the trailer, passed round the hind-quarters just above the hocks and pulled tightly. This method requires a minimum amount of labour (see Fig.26).

Mares with foals at foot, particularly young foals, can be encouraged to load easily if the bar at the front of the trailer is removed (as in Fig.27) to give the maximum amount of floor space; the foal is loaded before the mare and taken up to the front of the trailer. If the mare is kept as close to her foal as

101

Fɪɢ 27 Bar and partition removed ready for loading a mare with foal at foot

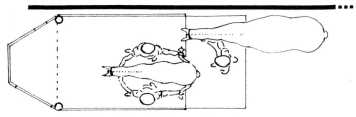

Fɪɢ 28 Load the foal first, and keep the mare close to her foal

possible all the time she will usually follow it into the trailer (see Fig.28). The bar is then replaced after the ramp has been put up.

Horses which are being shown or taken to sales must have their tails protected, otherwise they will rub the top of their docks during the journey. This will spoil their appearance and make the tail impossible to plait should this be required. Therefore it is customary to put tail bandages on horses before travelling. In order to keep tails clean it is also a good idea to cut a leg out of an old pair of tights and put the tail inside, securing it with a tail bandage put on over the top in the normal way. For extra protection in cases where horses are accustomed to wearing a roller, a tail guard can also be used. Coconut matting fitted to the back ramps of trailers and horse-boxes, as well as making the ramp more inviting for the horse to walk on to, provides a considerable amount of protection to its tail, hind-quarters and hocks during a journey. Further protection can be given by using hock boots.

Many trailers and horse-boxes have a slight space between the bottom of the partition and the floor. While travelling, horses usually keep their balance by standing with their legs apart, and so will often stand with their pasterns rubbing up against the bottom of the partition. Because of this, it is often wiser to apply stable bandages to a horse's legs before loading; where there is a solid partition in front of the horse, knee pads should also be worn.

Remember that it is just as important to get a trailer serviced regularly, as it is a horse-box. By doing so you will ensure that the braking system and hitch are maintained in good working order. The condition of the floor should also be checked at regular intervals to make sure there are no signs of excessive wear or rot; this is most important, as floors have been known to collapse. A strong safety chain should be fitted to all trailers.

As far as youngstock are concerned, trailers fitted with front unloading ramps are preferable as these do not teach young horses the annoying habit of running backwards out of trailers, immediately after loading. Horses can also have loading practice. With the centre partition removed, they can be walked up one ramp, through the trailer and down the other, then the centre partition can be replaced and the procedure repeated, until the young horse is quite used to the idea.

When driving a horse-box or vehicle which is towing a loaded trailer great care must be taken not to corner too sharply or slow down suddenly. The horses get a smoother ride if the gears are used as much as possible rather than the brakes alone.

CHAPTER FOURTEEN

Teaching horses to lunge and drive in long reins

LUNGEING, IN THIS context, means working the horse on a long rein in a circle, without a rider.

If you are not used to lungeing or long reining horses, practise on an older experienced horse. Never attempt to learn the art of lungeing and long reining using a young horse.

Lungeing has a dual purpose – it exercises the horse while developing its muscles and is a means of teaching obedience. The moment when lungeing can be started largely depends on the animal's physical development and condition. The length of time taken to teach each horse will depend on its character, age and temperament. Progress must be gradual and in line with the steady development of its physical and mental powers. Care should be taken not to over-tax a young horse.

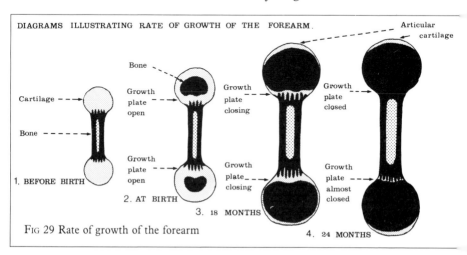

DIAGRAMS ILLUSTRATING RATE OF GROWTH OF THE FOREARM

FIG 29 Rate of growth of the forearm

The lungeing cavesson.

Young horses should not be lunged until their leg epiphyses have closed, which is between 18 months and 2½ years old. Up to this time work could cause inflammation of the growth plates immediately above the knee and hock joints, resulting in lameness.

For maximum control, it is essential that young horses are taught to lunge in a purpose-built ring. (See chapter 15). Never take a young horse into the middle of an open field and expect it to be attentive and safe.

The tack needed for lungeing and longreining consists of:

(1) Lungeing cavesson – this is, in effect, a strong headcollar with a low-fitting throatlash and well-padded noseband or preferably one of thick felt. The felt or padding is reinforced on the outside by a strong, hinged metal band carrying three stout rings. The heavier the noseband the more likely it is to rub a young horse's nose. A lightweight cavesson is therefore preferred.

(2) Lungeing rein – this is normally made from tubular cotton or nylon web. It should not be less than 25 feet (7.5m) long and must have a swivel and buckle or clip fastening at one end to prevent the rein from twisting and a loop at the other. The rein should not be too wide, otherwise it becomes very heavy when wet; about 1 inch (2.5cm) is ideal. Although the swivel and buckle must be strong it should not be heavy.

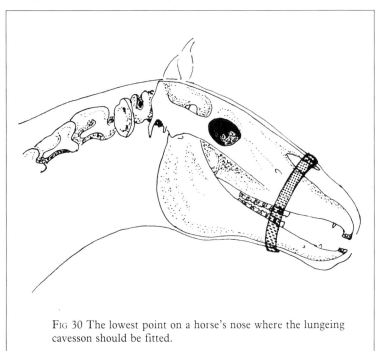

FIG 30 The lowest point on a horse's nose where the lungeing cavesson should be fitted.

The lungeing whip is used as an extension of your free arm to guide and control the horse.

(3) Lungeing whip – this is used as an extension of your free arm to guide and control the horse. It has a long handle and lash, together these must be the same length as the lungeing rein, otherwise the whip cannot be effective. Those made from fibre glass are preferred, as they are light to use, yet strong and durable. The junction between the handle and lash is inclined to wear, so should be strengthened with tape.

(4) Bridle – A simple straight bar, metal or rubber snaffle should be used. The thicker the mouthpiece, the milder the bit. Ensure that the bit is the correct size i.e. allowing about ¼ inch (0.65cm) between the lips and the bit rings either side; narrow bits pinch the lips. A straight bar snaffle is less severe than a jointed snaffle, with its 'nut cracker' action. A snaffle bit with long cheek pieces should not be used for breaking, as a lungeing or long rein could hook over the bit. The noseband and reins are not needed at this stage.

(5) Boots – young horses must wear boots on all four legs for lungeing and driving in long reins. Initially they are unbalanced and may knock themselves. Thick felt RANELAGH pattern polo boots which are at least 1 foot (30cm) deep are preferred. These are secured by four buckles fastening on the outside of the leg and include a 5" (12.5 cm) elastic, tendon support

(6) Side-reins – these should be made from leather with a loop at one end which attaches to the roller or girth and preferably a clip at the other end which fastens to the bit ring on the opposite side. Length adjustment is made by means of a buckle and strap. Ask your saddler to number the holes as both reins must be used the same length. There are two distinct patterns of side-rein. One is leather throughout, the other has a rubber or elastic inset. My own preference is for the former, as there is less danger that the horse will develop the habit of snatching at the reins.

(7) A roller or driving pad — this must be well padded and ideally fitted with 3 sets of terret rings. It should buckle on both sides for convenience. However, an ordinary canvas roller can be adapted for breaking. Two rings should be sewn on to the roller either side as well as one larger ring in the centre. The former to take a breast girth, or accommodate the side reins. An adjustable breast girth, fitted with clips rather than buckles either side, must be used whenever side-reins are omitted, otherwise the horse could buck through the roller. Some trainers also like to use a crupper. This must buckle either side, so that it can be opened and pass under the tail. Length adjustment is by means of a buckle and strap half-way along the back.

(8) Long reins – these are similar to lungeing reins, being made from tubular cotton or nylon web. Each pair should be the same length and not less than 25 feet (7.5m) long, with a light buckle or clip fastening one end and a loop at the other. The two reins must be quite separate and never joined to each other. Ideally a narrower web should be used than for lungeing reins, so that it will slide through the terret rings on the roller.

(9) Saddle – an old but sound saddle is normally used for breaking. It must be well padded, and of the correct size and width for the horse.

The throatlash must be tight, otherwise the outer cheek piece will be pulled forward into the horse's eyes. The side-reins shown in the photograph would be too short for a young horse: never ask for a head carriage at the trot, which is less than about 20° in front of the verticle.

(10) Gloves – essential if cuts and rope-burns are to be avoided.

To prepare the horse for its first lungeing lesson, put its bridle on. Run your hand down each each leg in turn as you put the boots on, talking to the horse to give it reassurance.

The cavesson noseband must be tight enough to ensure that it cannot move and rub the horse's nose. Most fit above the bit but some, like the Wels cavesson, are designed to go below the bit. The former is really preferred for young horses. Allow four fingers above the nostrils — the higher the noseband, the less control you have. If it is put on too low, it will interfere with the horse's breathing. The throatlash must be tight, otherwise the outer cheek piece will be pulled forward into the horse's eye. Both the noseband and throatlash, for comfort must be secured under the bridle cheekpieces. Attach the lungeing rein to the middle ring of the cavesson.

Most horses prefer to circle on the left rein (anti-clockwise), but not all. Just as some humans are left-handed, so some horses prefer the right rein (clockwise). To establish this, lead your horse round on the left rein; gradually step back, until it is moving round you in a small circle. Stop and repeat the procedure on the right rein. Note which direction your horse finds the easiest, then stay on that rein for the moment. As you pay out the rein, to encourage the horse to move forward take up a position in line with its hip. Hold the lungeing whip in your free hand. To slow the horse down or stop it, shorten the rein and move towards its shoulder and neck.

Use the same words of command you have been using throughout the horse's life: WALK-ON, trot being TE-ROTT, and for slowing down WA-ALK, long and drawn-out, then WHOA or HALT. Very young horses, those under 2 years old, should not be cantered on the lunge, as their legs are not fully developed at that age. Older horses can be given the command CAN-TER, when they are obedient at the slower paces.

The smaller the circle, the more control you have over the horse. However, turning too sharply increases the likelihood that the horse will knock its joints and legs by brushing or over-reaching. Therefore the sooner a larger circle can be used the better.

For the first lesson it is quite sufficient to spend 5 – 10 minutes on each rein or just teach the horse to go round you on its favoured rein. The words WALK-ON and WHOA should be introduced and obeyed. Initially the horse may not understand what is wanted. WALK-ON is usually easier for it to grasp, but WHOA (or HALT, if preferred), seems harder. To teach the latter, give the command coming into a corner, then you can move across and block the horse's exit, thereby enforcing obedience. Practise stops and starts, until the horse obeys once; make much of it and finish the lesson.

Lungeing lessons must be kept short, particularly in the initial stages when 10 – 15 minutes is long enough: young, immature, unfit horses soon become tired. Later the horse may be lunged for up to 45 minutes at a time.

When the horse is circling round you well in the one direction, he must be introduced to the other rein. This is where your

The open end of the lungeing rein is held in the hand. The rein itself should be neatly looped as shown in the photograph. This way, the person cannot put a foot through the loops while lungeing the horse and the rein can be played out smoothly without becoming tangled or knotted. Gloves must be worn to prevent rope burns.

111

troubles may start. Some individuals refuse to use this rein and 'dream up' a variety of methods to evade the trainer. Therefore, ensure that you can, as far as possible, enforce obedience.

The lungeing rein must be attached to the front of the noseband for maximum leverage and control. Place the horse on a small circle in a corner of the school. Using the walls to help you, take up a position behind the horse's inside quarter and drive it forward into the circle. Carry the whip behind you and only use it when necessary. Keep the horse calm; once it becomes flustered and 'loses its head' nothing will be achieved. If it is going to put up a fight, it will attempt to stop, half-rear and swing round, so it must be kept moving forward. Evasion calls for a very fast reaction on the trainer's part, an experienced trainer can often mind-read a horse before anything happens.

For this reason it is easier to work alone rather than with an assistant. The lungeing whip must be carried all the time. When the horse tries to evade you, the whip is used in conjunction with a strong downward pull on the rein to prevent the horse from swinging round and to drive it forward in the desired direction. Persistent cases that will not go forward may need the extra control afforded by long reins before they can be persuaded to lunge quietly in both directions. Once a horse is outwitted it usually gives in gracefully.

Most text books recommend that the trainer should fix one heel in the ground and so remain stationary when lungeing. With young inexperienced horses, this is not desirable. The trainer must be prepared to move round with the horse, mostly in a small circle, but sometimes to the rear of the horse, to drive it on; at other times towards the front to slow it down. It is better for the horse's limbs if it is allowed to make a large circle, the trainer walking round with it in a smaller circle to maintain control.

Experienced young horses which are balanced and obedient to the trainers' voice can be lunged as recommended. The lungeing rein should maintain a light even contact with the horse; a sudden pull unbalances the horse, but sometimes this cannot be avoided. The rein is always held in the left hand on the left rein, and in the right hand on the right rein. The whip is held in your free hand. Never lunge without a whip. The trainer must develop instant obedience right from the beginning — this is one of the objects of lungeing. The whip encourages forward movement and is used to keep the horse out on the circle.

Horses learn by cause and effect. Always praise it when it has done well. This way the horse will know what you require, but do make everything quite clear, using the same words and tone of voice each time.

When free to do so, most young horses like to examine the ground and some will walk or trot round with their heads down. In this position they can put a leg over the lungeing rein. A quick flick with the whip will regain their attention temporarily but permanent control can only be achieved with the roller and side-reins. A roller is essential for longreining and as an introduction to the rug and saddle.

The roller should be put on for the first time at the end of a lungeing lesson when the horse has been exercised. An assistant must hold the horse, while the trainer attends to the roller. Remove the crupper and breast girth. Slide the roller across the horse's back. Talk to it as you adjust and fasten the breast girth. Tighten the roller until it is just secure. Allow your assistant time to leave the lungeing area, then encourage the horse to move forward. On feeling the roller many horses buck and kick. Once it has settled, the horse should be lead back to it's loose-box. The roller and breast girth should be left on all night and only removed after the horse has been exercised the following day. The roller and breast girth are then fitted every day before exercise and removed when the horse returns to its stable. If desired, the crupper can now be fitted, as well as the side-reins. The side-reins must be adjusted on the loose side, otherwise the horse will be over-bent (go with its head behind the vertical), or resist the pressure by throwing its head in the air. In both cases its back will be hollow.

At this stage, one is trying to develop the horse's natural carriage and paces, therefore side-reins should not be attached too low on the roller. The reins either run to the bit rings on the same side or are crossed over the withers and pass to the opposite bit rings. The latter ensures that any pressure on the bit comes from as high a position as possible, and the reins cannot slide down.

Initially periods of trotting should not exceed 5 minutes at a time; when walking, the horse is allowed to relax. At the trot, the

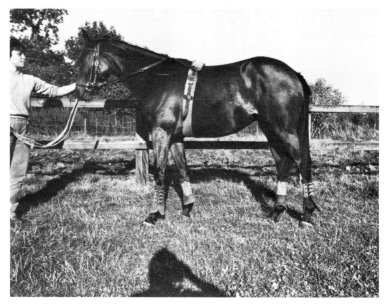

The horse tacked up ready for lungeing wearing a roller and side-reins. Since we are trying to teach the horse to move forward freely, the side-reins must not be shortened too quickly. Initially they should be long enough to allow the young horse freedom to stretch its neck at the walk, making little, if any, contact at the trot. As the horse becomes better balanced so it is able to use its back muscles and assume a more upright yet rounded form of self-carriage, then the reins can be shortened one hole at a time. By engaging its quarters, at this stage, the horse avoids lying on the bit. The side-reins should be lengthened between periods of trotting allowing the horse to stretch out and down at the walk.

trainer looks for a more rounded shape. The neck is stretched out and down. The hind feet should track up to the imprint left by the fore feet, causing the back and loin muscles to work and strengthen. The neck also develops. Lungeing must be carried out evenly on both reins.

The horse should be taught to halt on the circle and remain stationary until told to walk on. Always go out to the horse, never ask the horse to come in to you. Once learnt this can become an irritating habit.

More control can be achieved if the lungeing rein is fastened to the off-side bit ring, passed over the poll, through the near-side bit ring and back to the trainer. Alternatively the rein may be attached to the off-side bit ring, through the centre ring on the

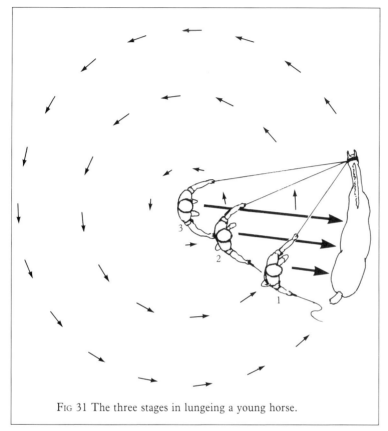

Fig 31 The three stages in lungeing a young horse.

roller and back through the near-side bit ring to the trainer. Many common evasions, such as refusing to lunge in both directions or attempting to turn away from the trainer out of the circle, cannot be fully prevented until the horse is put in long reins. In some cases long reins may have to be introduced from the beginning.

Longreining has many advantages over lungeing. The outer rein gives the trainer greater control over the horse and allows for more finesse in training. The use of the outer rein ensures that the hind feet follow in the same tracks as the fore feet. The horse can be worked in straight lines as well as on the circle. A good mouth and manners can be made before the horse is ridden.

The reins are attached to the bit rings below the side-reins; initially they are not passed through the rings on the roller for the

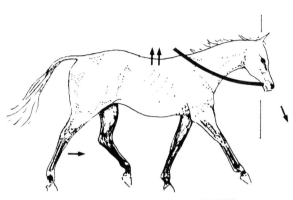

(1) ROUNDED AND RELAXED — TAIL SUPPLE (CORRECT)

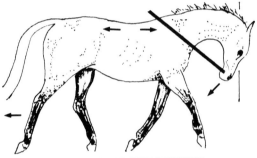

(2) OVER-BENT, BACK AND TAIL STIFF (INCORRECT)

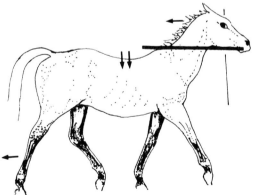

(3) HEAD UP, HOLLOW BACK AND TAIL STIFF (INCORRECT)

FIG 32 Possible effects of shortening the side-reins too quickly.

following reasons: if the trainer gets into a muddle and has to drop the outside rein, he can put both hands on the inside rein, if necessary, pull the horse round and commence lungeing until the horse can be stopped. If the horse gets a leg over a rein, it can be stopped, the rein dropped and pulled out from the front.

Longreining is introduced in stages, ideally extending over a period of some 8 weeks before the horse is backed.

Assuming the horse is accustomed to the roller, pass the outside rein across the top of the roller without using the rings. The inside rein comes directly to the trainer as before. The whip is held in the same hand as the outside rein. After the first lesson, the outside rein should be passed round the horse's quarters just above the hocks. This can be done in one of two ways:

(1) Pass the rein across the horse's rump and as it moves forward shake it down round the hocks. Some horses resent the rein across their backs.

(2) While holding the inside rein, take up a position towards the horse's hind-quarters. Ask your assistant to pass the outside rein behind the horse without touching it and hand it to you. Walk the horse on, keeping your outside hand low and the rein not too tight, otherwise it could rise under the tail, should the horse buck. If this happens, slacken off the trapped rein and it should eventually drop on to the hocks.

With both reins in operation the trainer is in much more control of the horse. Always place the horse on the rein it favours when introducing a new idea. Longreining may be used to cure horses which will only lunge one way. The outside rein acts in a similar way to the rider's leg in controlling the quarters and pushing the horse up into its bridle.

Work the horse as usual at the walk and trot on its favoured rein. At the walk move directly behind the horse from your position slightly to the rear of its inside hip. Keep the horse walking on, go back to your original position and repeat from time to time until the horse accepts the idea. A change of rein can now be introduced.

Drive the horse round the school using the reins as you would when riding. As you approach a corner feel the inside rein. Never pull back, but rather keep your contact and vibrate the rein until the horse relaxes its jaw and starts turning. Walk on across the school until you meet the opposite corner and turn on to the other rein. Take up your position slightly behind the horse's inside hip and you are lungeing in the other direction.

In the case of horses with a one-way-only complex, it is sufficient to drive them round the school on their bad rein before returning to work on the good rein. Gradually increase the number of times you use the bad rein and decrease the size of circle down to about 30 feet (15m). One day when the horse seems settled and is going forward freely on its bad rein, take up your position towards its inside hip and lunge it for one circle before driving it again. Gradually increase the number of circles until the horse will lunge equally well in both directions.

Changes in direction can now be introduced straight from one rein onto the other rein. The nearer one walks to the horse the more control one has, but care should be taken that you are not within range of the horse's heels. To change rein on the circle, the trainer moves in a straight line behind the horse bringing the horse round in a serpentine movement on to the other rein. The word CHANGE may be used.

After the first 3 weeks or so, a saddle may be substituted for the roller. Even though the horse has become accustomed to a girth round its middle, many still buck when they feel the saddle for the first time. The saddle should therefore be introduced towards the end of a lesson. Since the horse may buck and kick violently it is better to remove the stirrup leathers from the saddle before putting it on. Loose stirrups banging on its sides would only frighten the horse at this stage.

The side-reins should be attached just above the buckle guards. This will prevent them from slipping down. More stability is achieved in saddles with three girth straps if the buckles are fastened to the first and third straps. The side-reins are then passed round all three straps. If only the first and second are used, the side-reins must pass round these alone. The side-reins will need to be re-adjusted for length. It is unlikely that the position of the roller and saddle will be identical. Ensure that the side-reins are still slack and in no way pull the horse's head in.

118

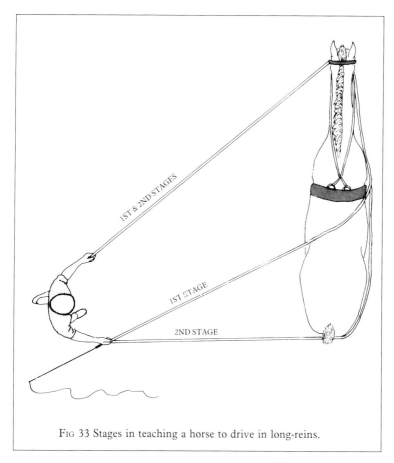

1ST & 2ND STAGES

1ST STAGE

2ND STAGE

FIG 33 Stages in teaching a horse to drive in long-reins.

From the second day the stirrup irons may be left on the saddle but they must be run-up and secured with the leathers to prevent them from sliding down. After about a week, towards the end of a lesson, the stirrup irons should be adjusted so that they are too high to make contact with the horse's elbows. They are then allowed to hang loosely and bang against its sides. Once the horse is used to the feel of the stirrup irons, they should be adjusted so that a rein passing through them will give a straight line from the bit to the trainer's hand, when driving the horse. The stirrup irons are then tied together under the horse's belly with a soft bandage, such as a tail bandage.

Throughout this period the horse should have been driven as

FIG 34 A horse ready to be driven in long reins.

much as possible, practising figures-of-eight and changes of rein to develop its mouth. Keep your hands low, and thus prevent the horse from tossing the reins over its head. However, this can now be prevented by passing the outer rein through the outside stirrup iron. The trainer is then in absolute control of the horse which can be driven round the farm or stud. Unfortunately, when working the horse on the circle, it is necessary to halt the horse and change the reins over with every permanent change in direction. It is unwise to work a young horse with both long reins through the irons, as it would be impossible to pull it round on to a circle in an emergency.

Before the horse is ridden it should be taught to rein-back. Work the horse in trot, then walk. To help the horse, drive it down one side of the school, keeping close and parallel to the wall, then halt. Check that the horse has its head low and is standing four-square. If not, walk on and halt once more. This time encourage the horse to walk on but instead of giving with your hands keep the contact and vibrate the inside rein with your little finger as the inside foreleg comes back and the outside rein for the outside foreleg. On no account pull back on the reins. Use the

120

The horse tacked up for lungeing with a saddle. The side-reins may be fitted as shown in fig. 34 or as shown above.

word BACK. Ask for one step only and eventually increase the number to three. Do not allow the horse to halt after stepping back, walk on without a pause. The sequence is; trot, walk, halt, rein-back, walk, trot. Ensure the horse keeps its back rounded; never let it reverse with a hollow back and its head in the air.

To avoid confusion in the horse's mind, reining-back should not be taught until the horse has a very clear idea of the commands for walk, trot and halt. The movement should only be practised once or at the most twice a day and then should be well interspersed with walk, halt, walk and trot to walk, halt, and walk on. The horse then only learns to rein-back on command. Half-halts can also be introduced at this stage.

Time should be allowed for the horse to strengthen its muscles on the lunge, before being asked to carry the weight of a rider. A period each day on the lunge should achieve a marked improvement in the horse's outline by the end of the first month. It should develop more crest, a stronger back, muscular quarters and second thighs.

Once the horse has settled each day ask for a steady working trot. Check that the hind feet track up to the imprint left by the

121

For comfort remove the stirrup leathers from the saddle. With the horse standing still, leg-up the rider to lean across the saddle. If the horse becomes upset the rider can slide to the ground, otherwise it can be led forward a little way. Always wear a skull cap when backing and riding young horses.

fore feet and that the neck is stretched out and downwards. The horse's tail should swing easily to the rhythm of the trot — this is the best guide that the horse is supple and using its' back muscles correctly. A stiff tail carriage indicates that something is wrong. At this stage a 60 foot (18 m) diameter ring should be used to avoid undue strain to the legs. The lungeing rein maintains nothing more than a light even contact with the horse, that is unless the horse is disobedient or offers some resistance.

Periods of trotting should not be prolonged on either rein and well interspersed with periods of walking. At this stage, if the horse is physically mature, the canter may be introduced. Two or three turns at the canter are usually sufficient. The horse should never be worked until its muscles feel tired, otherwise it will soon start resisting.

When the trainer decides that sufficient progress has been made, the horse may be backed. Some people use a large, well bedded loose-box. However, there is always the danger that the rider may be thrown against the roof or walls, so an enclosed schooling area or lungeing ring is preferred.

Ideally, time should be allowed for the rider and horse to become familiar with one another. Therefore, if the trainer is not going to back the horse himself the rider should be allowed to handle and lunge the horse for a few days before it is ridden. A very experienced rider *must* be used as it is essential that a fall is avoided. Should the horse succeed in dropping the rider it may develop a superiority complex and make a habit of putting its rider down.

Each day, pat and rock the saddle gently on the horse's back, so that the horse becomes used to the movement. On the appointed day, work the horse on the lunge in a saddle and bridle as usual.

Until required, the reins should be passed under the throatlash

If the horse is relaxed the rider can put his or her leg over the saddle taking great care not to touch the horse's hindquarters. Holding the neck strap, the rider must stay down in line with the horse. The horse may be walked forward. When the rider feels the horse is ready, with the assistant keeping the horse still, the rider may sit up slowly.

123

of the bridle and behind the stirrup leathers. A neck strap should be worn. Take the girth up gradually as the horse is worked. At the end of the lesson, halt the horse in the middle of the school. The trainer should stand to the near side, holding the lungeing rein. The rider should take up his position also on the horse's near side. Standing by the shoulder, he should take up the reins and some mane in his left hand and the waist of the saddle on the off-side in his right hand. He should rock the saddle slightly and talk to the horse. He then bends his left leg at the knee and the trainer slowly gives him a leg up, to lie across the saddle.

This exercise may be repeated several times before the horse is led forward with the rider leaning across the saddle. As soon as the horse accepts this new idea, the rider should move around cautiously on the saddle. Once this too has been accepted, the rider may put his right leg over the horse but he must keep his body down in line with the horse's neck. This should be done at the halt. If the horse remains calm it may be walked forward. When the rider feels that the horse is relaxed and when it is standing still, he may sit up very slowly. Care should be taken as some horses are frightened when they first see their rider at a higher level sitting up straight.

If the horse is relaxed it may be led round and the lungeing rein gradually paid out until the horse is being lunged as usual. All control remains with the trainer at this stage, the rider is merely a passenger. This may take several days to achieve.

During the next few weeks the rider gradually takes over from the trainer, substituting the aids for the words of command used up to this time. When the horse fully understands what is required it may be ridden off the lunge.

124

CHAPTER FIFTEEN

Notes on the lungeing ring

Y OUNG HORSES EXPERIENCE a certain degree of liberty at the end of a lungeing rein, so for safety they should always be lunged in an enclosed area. Once a fresh, strong horse gets away from you it will almost certainly try to repeat the performance and this obviously can be dangerous.

Ideally use an indoor school, close-boarded manège or ring. Failing this, fence off a quiet corner of a paddock. Since most fresh horses buck and kick on the lunge, the fencing used must be such that the horse cannot get a leg through or over the fence. Portable Weldmesh 'horse play pens' may be adapted for use as lungeing rings. Since their diameter is flexible they are ideal for schooling young horses. They are a relatively low cost, low maintenance method of providing safe fencing round a lungeing area.

The site chosen should be quiet and free from distractions, ideally in a sheltered position. It must be well drained and the surface sufficiently resilient to prevent concussion. A lungeing ring should be level and free from stones, which would break the hooves of unshod horses or cause bruised soles. Short grass can become slippery in both wet and dry weather. With constant work a bare track soon forms and the ground becomes too hard or too slippery. A man-made surface is therefore preferred.

The materials normally used for "all weather" surfaces include:

1. wood or rubber chippings or wood peelings and bark;
2. sand;
3. peat moss.

Wood chippings or wood peelings and bark may be obtained from

A portable weldmesh 'horse playpen' can be adapted for use as a lungeing ring, as well as providing a safe area in which stabled horses can have a buck, kick or roll.

forestry areas. Hardwood is preferred to softwood and some firms specialise in supplying wood chippings which have been treated to prevent rotting down. Many of these firms will also undertake to construct and lay the surface. Care must be taken initially as newly laid wood chippings or wood peelings tend to be slippery until they have been rained on or watered a few times. However, once they have settled they form a springy, even, light surface. Finely chopped outer covering from rubber electricity cable is also used with success.

Sand forms a loose, deep surface which soon tires a horse and may stress a young horse's legs.

Peat moss on its own is less effective than wood chippings or wood peelings and bark but liberal applications to grassland each year will lighten most soils, producing a springy surface.

The optimum size of a lungeing ring suitable for the early education of young horses, including thoroughbred yearlings, for walking and trotting only, is 40 – 45 feet (12 – 14m) diameter: a larger ring gives greater scope for disobedience; a smaller ring places too much strain on the horse's legs. For faster work a larger ring is essential and 60 – 80 feet (18 – 24m) diameter is considered ideal.

With use man-made lungeing ring surfaces tend to creep up the sides of the ring. Therefore, in order to contain the material, all rings must be close boarded to a height of at least 2 feet (60cms). In order to provide a level surface for each horse, the material should be raked over immediately after each horse has been worked or before the next horse is brought into the ring. All droppings must be removed.

Useful information and addresses

Qualifications in stud work

For anyone wishing to gain qualifications in stud work the following are some of the schemes available in the United Kingdom and Ireland:

(1) A post-graduate course in Equine studies is run by Prof. Ian Gordon at University College Dublin, Dept. of Agriculture, Lyons, Newcastle P.O., Co.Dublin, Ireland, and is open to suitably qualified people.

Several agricultural and technical colleges run courses on stud management including The Warwickshire College of Agriculture, Moreton Morrell, Warwick and W. Oxfordshire Technical College, Witney, Oxon. (the latter run a 3 year HND course in Equine Studies).

(2) The National Pony Society (Sec., Brig. J. D. Lofts, MBE) 7 Cross and Pillory Lane, Alton, Hants, organises examinations for candidates with one year's or three years' continuous stud experience — they also keep lists of studs which are normally prepared to accept working pupils. The examinations are for the Diploma in Pony Mastership and Breeding and for that of Stud Assistant. Both can be taken with or without riding. Details of the syllabus can be obtained from the National Pony Society at the above address.

(3) The English and Irish National Studs accept working students for a stud season. Those interested should write to: The Director, The English National Stud, Newmarket, Suffolk; or The Manager, The Irish National Stud, Tully, Co. Kildare, Republic of Ireland.

128

Useful addresses

Messrs. Weatherbys *(General Stud Book)*,
Sanders Road,
Wellingborough,
Northants NN8 4BX.

Hunters Improvement & National Light Horse Breeding
Society,
8 Market Square,
Westerham,
Kent.

Tindall & Son (specialists in stud stationery and
printing),
50 High Street,
Newmarket,
Suffolk.

The National Foaling Bank,
Meretown Stud,
Newport,
Shropshire. (Newport 811234)

Index